When to Say Goodbye— A Dog Story

Eleanor E. Fink

When to Say Goodbye—A Dog Story

ISBN 978-0-578-77001-7

To all our beloved canine companions—
Ebony, Windy, Brookie, Bo, Whiskers,
Elkie, Odin, and Zeus to name a few.

Acknowledgments

Love and gratitude to my husband, Stefan, for his support and for sharing the joys and heart-rending experiences described in *When to Say Goodbye—A Dog Story*. Special thanks to Betty and Bob, good friends, who at times took care of Ebony. Thanks to the following people for their expertise and assistance with reviewing and publishing this journal: Nancy Bryan, D.A. Spruzen, Lynne O'Connor, Ginny Glass, and Kimberly Martin of Jera Publishing.

Foreword

We love our pets. However, when they become ill, we face difficult decisions. Worst of all is deciding when to say goodbye. This journal is intended to help those who have a dog suffering from a serious illness. The information given here is not authoritative; the writer is not a veterinarian and disclaims any specialized medical knowledge. This is simply a personal account shared with those who face coping with a seriously ill dog as well as confronting the ultimate question of the right time to put the dog to sleep. Many may find the affection, enjoyment, and concern my husband, Stefan, and I expressed for our dog extreme. Nevertheless, I'm sure others will recognize the emotional bonds that form when your dog becomes an integral part of your family and, like a good partner, shares in and contributes to your everyday life.

In our case, our dog, Ebony, a large standard poodle, had a seizure and was taken to an emergency clinic at a time when we were on vacation in China. The vet told us Ebony was weak and had difficulty breathing and that, given her age (eleven years), the prognosis didn't look good. Upon our immediate return home, we began to face many complicated questions that left us uncertain. Our vet of many years told me to keep a journal to note when a seizure occurred and any changes in our dog's behavior. As we experienced more seizures and learned about what could be causing them, it struck me that other people undergoing similar experiences might appreciate comparing notes, sharing answers to tough questions, and hearing how we learned to handle challenging situations.

The internet is full of sad stories of painful experiences faced by people whose pets are ill. As our case showed me, many people find dealing with seizures difficult. A seizure is a disturbing sight to watch, especially if it's happening to a pet you love. Your dog may fall down and begin to frantically paddle with its legs in the air while gasping for breath. Its tongue will hang loose to the side, and its eyes will roll back. Typically, the dog will lose control of both bladder and bowels. The spasm seems to take an eternity when, in reality, it often lasts only a minute. Sometimes, the most difficult part follows the spasm, when the dog is confused and displays a frantic need to "walk off" the seizure.

Many people seem unsure about how to cope with repeated seizures and their dog's response or lack of response to medication. They may ask, "Is it time to put my dog down?" I can see the worry in their eyes whenever we talk about it. "My dog is taking so much medication and just sleeps." ... "Our dog has several clusters of seizures over a period of days and pees uncontrollably each time." ... "My dog can barely walk and hardly responds to us anymore." ... "Our dog just stares into space and doesn't seem to recognize us. I'm worried that we may need to make a decision soon."

At some point, you'll need to ask yourself whether the quality of life left to the dog is worth keeping it alive. However, just because your dog may have frequent seizures, lose bladder control, and sleep much of the time doesn't necessarily mean the end is near or that its quality of life is without joy. It's difficult to determine how long a dog exhibiting a pattern of seizures will live and what progressive changes will occur. Much depends on the cause of the seizures. When is the appropriate time to put a dog to sleep? What does putting a dog to sleep entail? Moreover, if you need to make that decision, how do you say goodbye?

I hope you'll find this book comforting and of some help in living with your dog's illness, enjoying the quality of life remaining and knowing when to shepherd them to the next stage.

How It All Began

I t was a boring hour-and-a-half ride. We passed one shopping mall after another with Wal-Mart, Kohl's, and Old Navy stores, and then finally turned off Route 66 into the country-side. Around a bend, we saw the remains of a once-beautiful barn and a giant silo tilted far to the side, ready to collapse at any moment. It was a sad reminder that this was once rolling Virginia farmland now filled with one crowded McMansion development after another. How ironic to live so close together far from a metropolitan area. We were excited about the journey because the mother and father would be there. After thirty more minutes of twisting roads, we arrived. Wagging tails greeted us.

We'd told ourselves we would only look. It had been two years, and we thought that perhaps it would soon be time. I had relocated to the metropolitan Washington, DC, area from Los Angeles, and now it made sense to share our lives with another companion again. The facility was clean and well kept. The proprietors were cordial but businesslike. We greeted the mother, who seemed to have a pleasant and friendly personality. The father was more mysterious and withdrawn. I observed that he stared at us with piercing eyes. Perhaps his reserve or mistrust was because the proprietors didn't own him; he was the sire of the litter. The owners' dog was the bitch.

The owners escorted us to an enclosed porch. They pointed to a dog in a kennel and told us she was the two-year-old offspring of the same parents. She was a knockout! There is something incredibly seductive about black standard poodles. She sat erect in her kennel, taking in everything about us with her lively eyes. Black silky locks fell around her face. They called her Wonder, and the name certainly suited her.

Not far from her kennel was a box containing the litter. Five eager pups had propped themselves up, wagging their tails to say hello. Three additional brothers and sisters were still asleep but started to yawn and open their eyes as we approached. The pups seemed to love people and wanted us to pick them up. It was as if they knew why we had come and were trying to say, "Hey, pick me."

The owner suggested we grab a few and go outside for a closer look. I wasn't even thinking about which ones I picked up. They were all happy and beautiful and seemed to love attention. After all, this was only a visit; we were only going to look. I had three, Stefan had two, and the owner grabbed two additional puppies. Our last dog, Windy, had been put down two years earlier when she reached age thirteen and suffered from liver disease. Windy had soft eyes and was very affectionate. I looked at the puppies to check which ones had soft eyes.

When I thought I'd found one, I showed it to Stefan, who was busy looking at the puppies he had selected. I don't know where she came from, but suddenly, one of the pups, who had evidently wandered away from the group, came romping back and jumped into the center of the pups and, in doing so, knocked the others down. She sat proudly in the middle of the heap, looking up at us with a self-satisfied grin. Stefan laughed and picked her up. The puppy immediately wrapped her front paws tightly around his arm, and that was it. At that moment, it was all over. She had chosen us!

A Good Match

We took her home with us that day. Puppies seem to love going home with their new owners. I see it at our neighbor's house where they foster puppies. We observe cars driving up, and later we see families leaving cradling little bundles of love. We named our new puppy Ebony because of her silky black curls. She was so attractive, Stefan would say, she could seduce a man anytime with her looks. She was a happy dog and had a unique grin and lively eyes that would challenge us to play and interact with her. She also didn't hesitate to look us straight in the eye and didn't flinch when we peered back at her. She made us feel happy just to be around her.

We had read several books about bringing up poodles. All mentioned the fact that poodles are incredibly smart. However, we had no idea how adept she'd be at getting inside our heads! She committed our habits and daily routine to memory. She knew when we were ready to take her for a walk and would start up ahead of us. Sometimes when I caught her watching me, I would walk up to her, bend down, and say, "Have you been sent down from outer space to record data on the habits of humans?"

It seemed natural to teach her some words, and before long, she had an extensive vocabulary. Several of the words we taught her come from the dialect spoken in western Austria in the Bregenzerwald, where Stefan grew up. For example, the word for *go outside* is *ussi, go around* is *ummi,* and *go up* is *uffi.* They were nice short words that were easy for her to learn. When she chased squirrels outside and they scurried to the other side of a tree, we would tell her, "*Ummi*," and she would circle the tree. When the squirrel scrambled up the tree, we said, "*Uffi*," and she knew to look up.

She loved it when I tried to outsmart her. I would intentionally do something unpredictable at play. She'd flash her eyes, grin broadly, sometimes lunge forward, and give me a quick kiss. She always managed to go right for my lips. On walks along the creek, people would stop and comment, "What a beautiful dog." She had an elegant prance, as if she were floating on air, and she could jump over a fallen log in a graceful leap as if she were light as a feather. We often marveled how she could be standing near the sofa and in one motion turn and leap elegantly onto it. She was energetic and agile, and could run like a racehorse. At the dog park, she turned heads when she raced about. Once, a dog owner, impressed with her speed, came up to us and asked, "Have you ever clocked her?"

We took her to a training course. She appeared bored throughout all the explanations, but when it came time to run through the lesson, she was always the fastest of the lot to get it right. The trainer would shout out, "The poodle got it again."

8

She grew to be taller than most female standard poodles. Yet I could cuddle her as if she were a puppy; she did not resist or pull away. In fact, when she was not quite a year old, a cutting board fell into the kitchen sink, making an unfamiliar noise. She noticed it immediately and appeared uncomfortable. I held out my arms and patted the sofa, and she leaped up and let me hold her. We called the noise "the kitchen monster." Every time the board fell, I would say, "Kitchen monster," and Ebony would automatically jump onto my lap for reassurance.

In addition to being tall with a deep chest, she had a long, elegant nose and long, silky ears. She was so statuesque that when she stood with one leg slightly forward, the pose reminded one of paintings of thoroughbred horses.

When we first brought her home, she followed us faithfully. We didn't need a leash. We have considerable woodland behind our house with several pathways. We started behind the house and toward the field, then up the path that runs to the top of the hill. I would look back and see her grinning as she followed, occasionally tumbling in the grass. She was only three months old.

It didn't take too long for her to start playing games, including "catch me if you can." It amused her if we coaxed her to come. Instead of behaving, she would dance around us. I'll never forget the dirty look she gave me when I finally put a collar around her neck and attached it to a leash. As I tugged, she resisted and looked at me as if to say, "How could you subject me to something so insulting?" Soon, however, she grew accustomed to the leash, and later, she appreciated the understanding we had that I would let her off the leash so she could run after squirrels, knowing she'd always come back.

We laugh about her first snow experience. We were excited to see how she'd react. She danced around like a falling snowflake—paws spread out, flexing up and down. It was hard to hold her back when we put her leash on. She jumped over the mounds of snow, sinking in and leaping out. About halfway around the trail, she began to shiver, holding up one paw and then the other. Snow always stuck to her fur and would cluster into ice balls between the webbed areas of her paws and toenails. She hadn't anticipated it would be so cold, so we turned home. One year, we bought her a red fleece blanket that fastened under her chest with Velcro. She enjoyed when I put it around her, knowing that we were about to go outside and that it would help keep her warm. She wore it proudly, and the red against her black curly fur looked stunning.

We loved her. At the time, our only disappointment was that she didn't bark. One day when she was about six months old, we heard a deep, guttural bark and wondered where it came from. We both looked at each other in amazement and went to the back room to find Ebony pressed against the window, barking at a squirrel. From then on, we often laughed when she threw back her head and barked. Who would have guessed she'd end up with such an impressive, husky voice?

It was fun watching her discover our house: early on, I found her trying out each sofa and chair. It amused me how she glanced my way before pulling herself up onto the sofa. She was just a few months old, yet she was already testing me to see how I would react. The small sofa became her all-time favorite. She'd prop up her head high on the pillows so that she had a good view out the window or toward the area where we were working. As she became full size, she filled the entire surface.

We placed dog beds in multiple locations so she could watch us. Although she had her own bed upstairs, she preferred to hop onto ours during the night. As she grew, we sometimes had to twist and move her around to make room for our legs. There was always a happy greeting with lots of kisses in the morning. She would bounce off the bed, follow Stefan downstairs for the first outside pee, and then back upstairs when he brought coffee. He always brought her a few cookies. She knew the routine and would leap onto the bed even when she was a good two feet away. She'd settle down between us like a lioness or sphinx, her long legs stretched out in front, waiting for her cookie while we read the newspaper.

Sometimes, she would get impatient, knowing that our reading delayed our morning walk. She'd raise her paw, strike down the newspaper that Stefan was holding, and look at us with expectant eyes. When we scolded her playfully and told her, "Not yet," she would sometimes edge forward and give us a kiss to make up for her impatience, or place her head on her paws and catch a few more winks.

Over time, we gave her several nicknames. On her kennel registration papers, she was Ebony Rose 4. Depending on the message we wanted to send her, we would tease or playfully call her Ebeler, Ebie, Muesler (meaning "little mouse"), Stinky Noodle, and Ebie Debie Doie.

We were challenged to find a suitable kennel to take care of Ebony when we went on trips. We had chosen not to crate her when she was a puppy. We found a place out in the country; what attracted us was their policy of matching dogs that got along well and letting them room together in a shed with a few beat-up sofas. Ebony loved labs and golden retrievers.

The pack played outside several times a day. The owner would send us emails letting us know how "Princess," as she called her, was doing.

It was always a joy to pick her up. Before we even got close to the shed we could hear Ebony howling and yipping as if she would tear down the walls and jump all over us. We were even more fortunate to have a good friend, Betty, who loved Ebony as much as we did and often took care of her. Betty enjoyed giving Ebony a bath, grooming and taking her on several walks a day, talking and playing with her. No matter how much Ebony loved Betty back, she always made a fuss when we dropped her off at Betty's house before leaving on a trip. She would try to follow us out the door and back into the car. Stefan would talk to Ebony in a soft tone and explain that we would be back soon. Then Ebony would settle down, and we felt better leaving. The reunions were ecstatic. Ebony would weave through our legs several times, eyes flashing, and kiss us all over our faces when we bent down to pat her.

The Incident

Ebony was eleven years old on September 30, 2010, and was as spry as ever. She understood us perfectly and was a great comfort if one of us was upset. If she heard a stressed tone in our voice, she would come over and give a kiss, hoping to make it better. We noticed over a period of some months that in the morning before she got on the bed for her cookies, she would lick her lips and swallow repetitively as if she were trying to clear her mouth or throat. We thought it odd, but she seemed comfortable otherwise. Ebony always knew when a trip was coming. She sometimes shot me a disappointed look when I got out the suitcase. We would get ready and then take her to Betty's house.

On the evening before our departure for Beijing, Ebony started twisting her mouth in a strange way as we walked down the front steps to take her to Betty. Right away, I felt uneasy because what I saw reminded me of our dog Brookie, who suffered from seizures later in life. When we left Ebony at Betty's house, she was unusually restless and looked pleadingly at us with wide eyes. It was heart-wrenching. Little did we know what was to take place subsequently.

It was exceptionally cold in Beijing in November. Much had changed since we'd been there in 2000 for a World Bank/ UNESCO Culture Conference. For one thing, the bicycles were all but gone, replaced by cars. We spent two days visiting the Forbidden City, Summer Palace, and Great Wall and many other sights. On the evening of the second day, I returned to our room after an exceptionally good massage. When I opened the door and saw Stefan's face, I knew something must have happened to Ebony. He told me that Betty had called. She'd cried over the phone, telling him that Ebony had had a seizure just as she was starting out for a walk. Betty had managed to get Ebony back inside, but when Ebony fell over again, she became worried and called our vet. Unfortunately, it was late Saturday afternoon and the offices were already closed. The outgoing message said that if the call was an emergency one should contact the emergency clinic and gave the number. Betty called the clinic and took Ebony there with the help of a neighbor. The clinic immediately put Ebony on monitoring devices and intravenous medication.

I called the doctor, who sounded pleasant, but she indicated that Ebony's condition was very serious. Her breathing was not good, and she emphasized that, given Ebony's age, she might not pull through. We were shocked because Ebony had been healthy and hadn't shown any signs of problems except for the twisting of the mouth and licking her lips. It was also worrisome because we'd lost Brookie, a poodle-schnauzer mix, because of seizures. We had boarded her with our vet and provided instructions to give her medication. While we were away, she had a bad series of seizures and the vet's staff on duty put her on a higher dosage of medication administered intravenously. She never really recovered after that episode.

We were scheduled to go from Beijing to Xian, and then Shanghai. I had told the doctor that, should Ebony pass away, we wanted her body kept until we returned. We both felt numb after the call, and there were no words to express our sorrow. Although we tried to sleep, I turned on the lights after ten minutes and said, "Do you think we can enjoy the rest of the trip not knowing what Ebony may face?"

"No," Stefan replied. We agreed that I would call United Airlines to see if we could get on a return flight the next day. Fortunately, all my work-related travel provided me with high-level status on United. United was very understanding, and we were able to book a return flight promptly. Then I called Betty and told her we were coming home.

She said, "I know Ebony will be happy to see you."

Beijing Airport is a marvel, with gigantic open spaces. However, we moved through the day and the plane trip to San Francisco in a daze. Once you get to full altitude on trips to and from Asia, it can get cold. Since we were still in semi-shock, it was particularly chilling. The down comforter didn't help. I tried watching one movie after another, but I found that what I was watching wasn't registering. Instead, I had one memory flash after another about our time with Ebony over the past eleven years.

Stefan said to me, "If only we could have her with us for another few months."

We could see her beautiful face and long nose. I thought about her playfulness and how she often would come up to me while I was working on the computer and either snatch a surprise kiss or bump up my hand from the keyboard. Then she would give me that expectant look and grin. I seldom could resist and would stop what I was doing and go out to play with her.

We recalled how Ebony would look directly at you when you spoke to her. I could say something, and she would turn to listen, and then Stefan would say something and she'd turn toward him. If five people spoke to her, she would always look at the person speaking. It amazed visitors. I also thought about how she protected me. I recalled inviting neighbors to the house. There was a high level of chatter going on. When I looked over at Ebony, she was sitting like a sentry, making sure I was OK.

When our plane arrived in San Francisco, I called the vet at the emergency clinic. It warmed my heart somewhat to hear that Ebie was doing better, and the vet asked what they could feed her. Then I called our regular vet and told him what had happened. He told us she probably has idiopathic epilepsy (a condition not uncommon in dogs, for which there is no apparent underlying cause) and that we should bring her to his office when we got back. His tone was also encouraging. Then I called Betty, who said she would pick us up at Dulles and take us directly to the emergency clinic.

The rest of the trip was a fog.

When we arrived at Dulles and met Betty, she talked about the incident and how scared she had been when Ebie had collapsed the second time inside the house, falling against the refrigerator. She had enlisted a neighbor to help her lift Ebie and get her into the car. Ebie had resisted.

When we got to the clinic, we were taken to a waiting room. The attendant explained that Ebie had been receiving a lot of medication and would be very weak. We'll never forget the next moments. They brought Ebie on a leash. She was lethargic, plodding along with her head hanging down, carefully placing one foot in front of the other. Then she sensed us, and immediately her tail started wagging fast. She came to us and went right through our legs, back and forth the way she did whenever we were reunited. She was so happy to see us that we thought she might have a heart attack from the excitement. We squatted down, petted her, and talked to her, expressing how glad we were to see her. Her response gave us some hope that it might be OK and maybe she would recover.

The doctor's assistant went over the medication with us. They had given her a seizure medication called Zonisamide. The dosage consisted of several pills amounting to 350 mg a day. I recalled that Brookie had taken phenobarbital.

We got Ebony into Betty's car, and I sat in the back seat with her. During the trip home, Betty kept looking back, shaking her head, saying, "She sure is something. I cried as much for her as I did when my mother died."

Ebie was resting her front paws and head on my lap, and every now and then, she lifted her paw and dropped it on my hand as if trying to tell me she was sorry. But she didn't have to say anything. I kept telling her, "I know. I know. It's OK. We're going home. We love you."

Dogs often seem embarrassed if they cause you grief. If they cry out in pain and you respond emotionally, they seem to want to apologize for upsetting you. We wanted Ebony to know that, no matter what, we loved her. When we got home, we got her on the bed, and the three of us had a good night's sleep. We were together again.

"Pick me"
Ebony's brothers and sisters

As she grew bigger, she filled the entire small sofa

Pretty girl with long curly ears and elegant nose

Thoroughbred horse pose

"Any rabbits down there?"

Corkscrew curls

JOURNAL

December 2010 to January 2014

TRIALS

December 2010—December 2011

New Beginnings

Ebony seems reasonably fine. We saw our vet, who raised an eyebrow when we told him we had returned from China because of Ebony. I mentioned that the doctor at the emergency clinic told us that Ebony might not survive. Our vet shook his head and pointed out that emergency clinics treat animals' problems as worst-case scenarios. He emphasized that Ebony simply seems to have had a seizure. He informed us that many things cause seizures, including cancer and brain disorders; he also said that it wasn't uncommon for dogs to have epilepsy, especially poodles. Sometimes the condition is genetic, what is called *idiopathic epilepsy*, which means that the cause isn't known. He said, if his office had been open on Saturday afternoon, he would have told our friend Betty not to worry and would have prescribed seizure medication and sent Ebony home.

He examined Ebony, testing her responses. She grinned at him, acting attentive and alert. He concluded that Ebony might indeed have idiopathic epilepsy, which means she'll continue to have seizures but could live out her life. Looking at the medication the clinic had given her, he said he probably would have prescribed something else. Since they had started her on Zonisamide, it made sense to continue. He suggested radically reducing the dosage to 25 mg twice a day to see what happens. He also suggested keeping a journal to record any incidents of seizures and changes in behavior.

We felt relieved that Ebony might be able to live out her life with idiopathic epilepsy. We also welcomed his recommendation to reduce the dosage because we associated excessive medication with the shortening of Brookie's life. We wondered to what extent emergency clinics exaggerate conditions. We were still taken aback by the bill for the emergency treatment. The sum for Ebony's two-a-half-day stay came close to the cost of the airfare and hotels in China. Over the next few days, Ebony was even more herself, especially after we reduced the medication, which made had her sleepy. (Much later, we learned that a higher dosage is recommended for a dog her size.)

December 15: Back to Normal

With the reduced medication, Ebony is running and happily dancing in circles again. She jumps onto the small sofa and watches us out of her twinkling eyes as we go about our daily routine. When she climbs onto the sofa and sinks down into the pile of pillows with only her head appearing on top of her front paws, we often think, despite her size, that she looks like a little mouse. In fact, we sometimes call her "muesler," a variation of *muesli*, a dialect word from the western province of Austria near the Swiss border, which literally means, "little mouse."

We're back to normal behavior, including our routine when I come home at the end of the day. After a happy greeting with Ebony weaving in and around my legs, I head upstairs, and she dashes up the steps with me. Sometimes, we almost fall over each other racing to the top. Once upstairs, she sits and waits patiently until I change into casual clothes. Her eyes are always all over me as if to say, "Hurry up." Finally, I get on the bed and with great anticipation, she leaps onto it as well.

Next, we start to rough around. Ebie lowers her head with her rear end in the air and growls. Then, using my fingers, we play the mind game. We know she studies us and that she is aware of our next move before we sometimes are!

I therefore challenge her by moving fingers in unexpected ways. We share some special moments when she concedes that I do something out of the norm and "outsmart" her. I move my fingers around her head and open mouth, sometimes circling right and sometimes reversing and going left. With her mouth hanging open, her eyes faithfully follow the pattern up and down and around. She's waiting for the right opportunity to catch my fingers.

As I start to vary the pattern, she sometimes steals a quick glance at me as if to say, "How dare you?" When I rush my fingers over her tongue and open mouth, she snaps her mouth shut to catch my fingers. If she gets them, she wins. Although her sharp crocodile-like teeth appear dangerous, she never hurts me. As soon as her teeth feel my hand, she stops. The more I "outsmart" her with my movements, the rougher it gets. She becomes furious. The gold in her dark brown eyes flashes as her lips curl back in a savage-looking snarl. She barks to protest. She is always disappointed when we stop playing. Eventually, I stretch out, she with me. Then play turns to stroking, and finally, we catch a quick nap before dinner.

December 17: We Felt the Bed Shaking

It was 4:00 a.m. Ebony was having a seizure and was urinating in pulses. We bolted upright fast. Her feet were initially stiff, and then they started paddling. It was over almost before it started. She was breathing heavily, and her tongue was hanging to one side. When the seizure stopped, she started coughing as if something were caught in her throat. As she coughed, some bright spots of blood appeared. In anticipation of a seizure, we had started to cover the end of the bed with a plastic shower curtain and an old cotton sheet on top. Both could be easily washed.

December 19: Another Short Seizure in Her Sleep

It was at 4:30 a.m. Again, her tongue hung to the side, and she was breathing heavily. This time, there was no blood. When I happened to call out Stefan's name, Ebony immediately turned to look at me, despite the fact that she was still emerging from the seizure. Once it was over, she wanted to stand on her feet, but her legs were like rubber. After a few minutes, she was able to get up, and we walked her around to calm her down. We soon learned that walking her around after a seizure was an important part of the event.

Later that morning, I called our vet and asked if we could increase her medication to 50 mg twice a day, and he agreed.

December 21: Zonisamide

We observe that Ebony shakes her head a lot and has tremors. Sometimes, her head and eyes twitch. She also licks her lips as she had done for several weeks before we left for China.

Although our vet has suggested Ebony's condition might be idiopathic epilepsy, we remain concerned about what causes her seizures. Could it be a tumor or other illness? I read that epilepsy in dogs is very similar to what occurs in people. We had seen Brookie go into seizures several times. Her mouth and body would twist in a tight spasm while her legs paddled frantically in the air. I checked Zonisamide on the internet. Unlike the phenobarbital we had given Brookie, Zonisamide is a medication primarily used on people. It appears that there are some Zonisamide tests being conducted on dogs in Germany, but as yet, there's little information about its success with animals. The articles mentioned that Zonisamide is supposed to have fewer side effects than most of the other medications used to control seizures in dogs. I also read that if a dog has a brain tumor, chances of survival after surgery are very low. Therefore, we're keeping our fingers crossed that she'll live out her life with the seizures and we'll figure out how to handle them.

We discovered that Walgreens has a medication plan for dogs. The cost is thirty dollars a year, but you save that and more filling the first prescription. Buying at least a hundred pills saves even more.

December 24: A Very Special Christmas

The best present is having our Ebony with us, and although she's having seizures, she's as attentive and playful as always. When we were on the return flight from China thinking about the dire prediction from the emergency clinic, we hoped Ebony would be with us for at least another month. Now we're happy and much relieved that she isn't going to die after all. So we have prepared for Christmas as always.

Every year since she was a puppy, I loosely wrap a few presents for her and place a cookie or rawhide stick inside the wrapping with a toy. Of course, she smells the treat and will pick up the present and shake it around and then firmly place one paw on top and tear off the wrapping with her teeth. Usually during the process of opening the present, the toy squeaks, which excites her even more. When she finishes opening the wrapping, she tosses the toy into the air and then for next thirty minutes serenades us with squeaks. After many years of watching me place presents under the tree, Ebony always knows which are hers. Typically, I wiggle my finger and tell her not to touch her presents until we're all ready. From time to time, as we prepare Christmas Eve dinner, we hear a squeak, and then we know she was too anxious to wait.

Although Ebony has several favorite toys, especially the little squirrel and rabbit, she always chooses to play with the new ones for the first few weeks.

December 25: Christmas Day

There are thick snow flurries. I open the back door, and Ebie dashes outside and then, like a gazelle, zigzags through the field with her head high.

We're going for a walk along the trail behind the house. With some snow on the ground and chill in the air, Ebony seems invigorated. She trots up to the top of the hill. We often share some special moments at the top, surveying the woods and listening for the sound of approaching squirrels. When we come across deer, it's always a surprise. I sometimes find that I'm looking right through them as if they're invisible. Of course, Ebony always spots the deer and then chases after them. Now as we stand at the top of the hill, Ebony holds her head high and sniffs the air. The cold wind sweeps back the fine cashmere-like fur on her face and the corkscrew fur of her winter coat. With her eyes half closed, she embraces the cold wind like a Shetland pony.

December 26: Hearty Appetite

Up to age eight, Ebony had been a fussy eater, often leaving food in her bowl. While she was staying at Betty's a few years back, Zeus was there. Zeus, a large Doberman, belongs to Betty's friend Bob. Zeus always has a good appetite and at first tried to finish Ebie's food after cleaning his own bowl. Ebie put him in his place right away. After becoming good friends, Ebony picked up from Zeus the practice of always finishing her dinner. Over time, we noticed how much the two dogs copy each other. Now we notice that Ebie wants more food than usual and is eager to eat morning, noon, and night. I recalled that my father's dog Elkie, a beautiful German shepherd, had developed an eating disorder owing to a brain tumor. Her appetite had increased so much that she even tried to open a can of dog food with her teeth. Eventually, she became blind and bumped into things. It broke his heart when he made the difficult decision of putting her to sleep. The vet had told him the tumor was inoperable.

December 27: All Is Fine during the Day

As I work at my computer, I hear Ebony coming up the staircase and then the tapping of her toenails on the wooden floor leading into my office. She has that smile on her face, as if she's laughing and ready to engage me in something. I turn in my chair to greet her. She puts her head between my legs for me to rub it and then snorts with pleasure. However, at night, Ebony is beginning to display a different attitude. She's very quiet, she repeatedly licks her lips, and she vigorously shakes her head. Often, we see tremors.

December 28: Another Seizure

Ebony had a seizure at 9:10 p.m. after going outside before bed. She'd been exceptionally hungry at dinner. Several months ago, she developed the habit of stroking my or Stefan's arm with her paw to tell us she wants more to eat. She watches the food on our plates even after finishing everything in her bowl. She also seems unusually nervous. We had a leftover beef bone and gave it to her. Stefan always holds the bone while Ebie rips off the meat.

When Stefan took her outside, he noticed her mouth twitch, and then the seizure started before they could reach the door. It seemed long, but it probably was only a minute. After heavy panting, she was eager to stand up. She reared on her hind legs, putting her front paws on Stefan's chest. It was difficult to hold her down. Then she had wrenching coughs. Fine blood spattered from the deep coughing. Stefan walked her around the house. She sniffed intensively and finally quieted down. She wanted to stick close to us and sleep on the bed. She slept solidly between us during the night, sometimes turning on her back with her feet in the air. We often marvel at how she sticks her feet in the air like a cat. Poodles have deep chests, and when they lie on their backs, it's difficult for them not to fall to the side. Their legs have to be perfectly spread out to maintain balance. From time to time, Ebony loves to rock from side to side in this position snorting with pleasure. We call this routine "snortling."

Dec 29: A Good Morning

After the attack last night, we awoke to the sound of Ebony "snortling." She jumped off the bed and began a good stretch. When Stefan called her, she rushed down the stairs. She bolted out the door like a kangaroo bouncing up and down and leaped over a fallen tree to chase a squirrel that had quickly scrambled up a tree and had then jumped to the next branch. We gave her the medication and went for a walk down by the stream. As usual, people stopped to admire and pet her. She's a knockout with her winter-length corkscrew curls that spiral off the top of her head. Her fur is fine and very soft to the touch, like angel hair or cashmere. I remember, when she was eight months old, our neighbor across the street would call Ebony over just to run her fingers through Ebie's fine fur. When we took Ebie for her first haircut, our neighbor scolded us for not saving the cut-off fur for stuffing a pillow.

Dec 30: Fun and Games

Ebie is fully herself. She even barks at me while I'm working at the computer to tell me she wants attention. We played hide-and-seek, and she was sharp as a tack. Makes you wonder. If she has a brain tumor, it certainly isn't showing in her attentiveness. I hid her new toy and then called her into the room to find it. She loves this game and comes trotting in with a smile on her face, eager to find the hidden toy. She found it right away. The second time she came in prematurely and saw where I was standing. Naturally, she went to that area first and again found it quickly. The third time was more of a challenge. She came in and sniffed the top of the bedroom dresser. She looked in all the places where it had been before. Then she carefully scanned the top of the tall bookcase (the fact that dogs even think of looking way above eye level amazes me). Finally, she saw the toy hiding behind a plant and trotted over to fetch it. I always clap when she finds the toy and tell her "Good girl" or "Smart doggie." She loves being praised, and her eyes flash in excitement.

December 31: Signs of Insecurity

Typically, when we retire upstairs to the TV room, Ebony settles down on the lambskin rug in front of the television. I say "settles down" because she does a corkscrew dance, going around and around in circles several times until she folds her legs and reclines. Frequently, she turns on her back and starts snortling, rolling back and forth.

Last night, she seemed insecure and crawled behind Stefan's chair. I came over to pet her, but she avoided me by pushing me away with her legs. When she slept, I could see her eyes twitch and occasionally her body jerked as if electrical currents ran through her.

January 1, 2011: New Year's Day

It's important to administer the medication every twelve hours around the same time. Therefore, Ebony gets a pill at 7:00 a.m. and then at 7:00 p.m. Last night after receiving her pill, she seemed very insecure. She was sitting erect in her statuesque pose, but shaking slightly. Her front legs seemed weak, and she kept licking her lips. Her eyes looked glazed, and she seemed to stare right through me. She tried to raise her paw, perhaps to tell us something. We carefully took her upstairs. She slept behind Stefan's chair and later came onto the bed. In the morning, she seemed completely normal. She came in a little while ago and put her head between my knees for a head massage. She snorts and grunts, indicating she wants more.

January 4: Invisible Deer

It's interesting that at night when we retreat to the TV room, Ebony spreads out in front of us again in the open rather than squeeze into the tight space behind our chairs. She sleeps and eats well and wants to play. When I came home yesterday afternoon, she trotted as always to the door and snorted as she weaved in and around my legs. She's a big girl and sometimes throws me off balance. I notice that she stills shakes her head back and forth as if something were tickling her ears. I wonder if it could be ear mites or if there's a tumor. We went for a walk although it was nearing dusk. Wind-whipped flakes were slicing through the dimming light. The falling snow began to dance in swirls, first coming sideways, then reversing and spiraling upward.

As we walked up the trail, I glanced at the silhouette of the leafless tress along the hillside. Unknown by me initially, there were a herd of invisible deer several feet in front of us, their thin silhouettes blending in with the trees. Ebie saw them and galloped up the side of the hill. I only realized they were there when they bolted to escape her chase, their white tails disappearing in the snowy landscape.

January 11: Lyme Disease and Saying Goodbye

While deer are lovely to observe, so elegant and naïve, they bring ticks. Two years ago, we came home after an Easter service, intending to take Ebony for a nice long walk, but found her limping badly. Her right front leg kept caving in. Our vet immediately guessed it was Lyme disease and ran a blood test, which came out positive. She was placed on strong antibiotics, which seemed to help her. The limping went away. Nevertheless, we have to run blood tests on her every year. Our vet told us that the disease never completely goes away and can recur.

Recently, I came across articles that link Lyme disease with seizures. We made an appointment with our vet to talk about it. Ebony's right front leg has been caving in again and sometimes when she falls forward, she has a seizure. It's the leg that was partially shaved for the IV when she was at the emergency clinic. However, our vet doesn't think Lyme disease is the cause of her seizures. He keeps saying she just has idiopathic epilepsy.

Before leaving, I observed a woman at the front desk crying. I heard her say, "It's so difficult to say goodbye." I guessed what had happened and went over to sympathize. I shared that we had to say goodbye to the two dogs that we had before Ebony. Brookie was the mother, and Windy was her puppy. I say puppy, but Windy reached aged thirteen. The woman commented how each dog is so special and said there will never be another like the one she just lost. Then she stopped to compose herself and added that there will be room in her heart for another dog when the time is right.

January 12: Fairyland

It snowed overnight, leaving two powdery inches on the ground. Looking out from the eight-foot-high bedroom windows, it's a fairyland—virgin and peaceful, except for the squirrels running up and down the tree. We head for a walk in the pristine air. Ebie loves the snow and dances around in it, leaving white powder on her nose and big paws. She laughs and her eyes beg for some fun and play.

A rosy light gradually sweeps the blanket of snow. There are beech trees ahead of us that still have a few remaining golden leaves. The sound of their rustling creates a moment of magic as if we're entering a fairy kingdom and gold dust will soon drift across our path.

January 13: Two Attacks

Lately, we have observed that Ebie seems unstable: The problematic front leg keeps caving in. It is for this reason we thought she might have a recurrence of Lyme disease. In addition, her hindquarters seem stiff. When she turns quickly, she seems less nimble, and stumbles.

We had a surprise at 2:30 a.m. After more than two weeks, Ebie had a seizure. She didn't cough after it was over, but she was very restless and wanted to sniff everything and move about. We felt badly to see her go through it, despite the fact that veterinarians claim that pets have no memory of what happens.

I spent most of the day at work. When I came home, Ebie greeted me at the door and stepped outside to check what was happening in the neighborhood. Our house sits on top of a hill with a broad view up and down the street. I went to my Pilates class, and when I came home an hour later, Ebie was curled up like a woolly caterpillar in my chair. I didn't disturb her. She had already eaten and finished everything in her bowl (dog food mixed with homemade beef broth).

At 9:00 p.m., she had another attack when Stefan took her out for the last walk before bed. She was coming back from the lot next to our house when she began twisting her mouth and then fell. It was dark, and there was still snow on the ground. I was upstairs and heard Stefan call out. By the time I got to them, he was trying to drag her into the house. She was covered with snow and felt ice-cold. She was breathing heavily, her tongue hanging out of the side of her mouth, and her eyes were dilated. We kept stroking her and telling her it was OK and that she was a good dog. We wanted to make sure she knew we were there for her and that what was happening wasn't because she had done anything wrong.

She was very restless coming out of it, more than usual. It took at least thirty minutes before she settled down. We took her upstairs. For the first time that I can recall, she hesitated to climb the steps. Once upstairs, we kept her with us in the TV room. She was still restless and wanted to pace. She seemed particularly curious about something in the front of the house and nervously looked out the French doors by the balcony. We checked, but there was nothing we could see. She began to sniff every piece of furniture and surface in the bedroom intensely. From time to time, she even looked up toward the ceiling as if a poltergeist were about to emerge. Then she finally settled down. We decided she should go on her bed, so I took her to the bedroom. I got in bed, and she immediately jumped up and snuggled up alongside me. She wanted the comfort of being close. We left her there. The night passed.

January 16: Snortling for Joy

At 5:30 a.m., Ebie got up and looked out the window. It is a crisp, cold day. She got on her back and started snortling. We went for two walks. First, I took her up the trail behind the house. I was ahead and looked back as she trotted along. There was lots of steam coming out of her mouth as she sniffed the side of the trail analyzing the spoor of deer, fox, and other dogs.

Our second walk was along the creek. Stefan and I stopped to talk with a young woman with a golden retriever named Basil about the plans to widen the creek. At the end of the conversation, I mentioned Ebony's epilepsy.

The young woman looked shocked and said, "But she looks so healthy. I hope that never happens to Basil."

I replied, "Well, enjoy every day."

January 17: Playful

Ebony makes you feel happy just being around her with her laughing smile. She brings me toys and nudges me to play with her as she draws me in with her eager eyes. The little rabbit and squirrel are her favorites. She even barked at me to stop typing on my computer and take her for a walk.

However, at night, she jerks a lot. We were sure she was going to have another seizure last night, but when morning came she dashed around outside and didn't want to go inside. I couldn't help but think how important it is not to overreact. Looking at her now having fun, I know it helps to let her enjoy normal routines. I hope we'll know when the time is right to make changes.

January 21: Outdoor Games

All has been well, except we notice that Ebony twitches frequently. She enjoys her morning walks, as do we. She knows when we turn the corner of the trail behind the house that the walk is over. Typically, she starts jumping, trying to draw us into a game to delay going inside. Sometimes, we give her a glove, and that really sets her off. She throws the glove in the air and scrambles to fetch it. If I pick it up, she looks up at me eagerly, hoping that I'll throw it in the air again. Lately, I've been extending our walk by going to check the new bird feeder by Stefan's office. When Ebie sees me headed for the side of the house instead of the back door, she gallops alongside me, looking up with that smile. When we get to the birdhouse, she quickly goes to the front steps and sweeps the neighborhood with her eyes. I turn around, and instead of going into the house, I head for the shed. Again, she gallops along, thrilled that we have extended our walk, wondering if there's more to come.

January 22: Another Seizure

Last night, Ebie seemed very quiet. Since we didn't see any jerks for a while, we thought perhaps the seizures had come to an end and all would go back to normal. However, when Stefan took her out for her evening walk, she had one. She went down the hill of the lot next to our house, stopped, and stared into the night. He saw her head roll back and forth, and then she collapsed. The temperature was dropping into the teens. He couldn't lift her, but managed to get her on level ground behind our house. He called me, and I came out.

She was thrashing around and then breathing deeply. When she got out of it, she wanted to jump up on her hind legs, and in that moment, she hit Stefan in the mouth and cut his lip. We got her in, and Stefan walked her around by the collar for ten to fifteen minutes until she finally quieted down. She was very weak, and when she sat looking at us, she began to sway from side to side. We took her upstairs. She wanted to keep walking, but we confined her to the TV room with us. She went to the French doors by the balcony, spotted something outside, and started barking. We checked and had to squint until we saw that people were getting into or out of a car across the street. Her long-distance eyesight certainly is sharp. Gradually, she was ready for bed. There were no more incidents that night, and in the morning when we took her for our morning walk, she enjoyed every minute of it. A little while ago, she picked up her Christmas toy and brought it over to me. I threw it, and she caught it right away with precision. I hope this is just idiopathic epilepsy.

Experimental Treatments

I read an article that said veterinarians can't find physical problems in pets that have idiopathic epilepsy when they aren't in the process of a seizure. All the blood tests, all the X-rays and examinations come back normal. Sensing this is going to be a challenge, I keep reading up on epilepsy. I found an interesting piece of information in a philanthropy newsletter about a doctor in Australia who received a grant for a clinical study on triheptanoin, a triglyceride edible oil that may be effective as an add-on treatment for adult epilepsy patients. By talking with a nutritionist, I discovered that coconut oil is a triglyceride. The description of the treatment mentioned that a special high-fat, low-carbohydrate diet (ketogenic) was also recommended in some cases. We're considering trying this on Ebony along with her medication.

January 23: Hide-and-Seek

Temperature got up to twenty-nine. We went for a quick walk up the trail and later down to the creek. Ebie is very strong. Her hind and front legs no longer act weak, and she seems very firm on her feet. She trots alongside me, head up like a show dog. Stefan and I often play hide-and-seek with her when we're out walking. Usually, Stefan is far ahead, and Ebony races to catch up. When there's enough distance between us, I hide behind bushes or a tree, and then I let out in a loud high-pitched yip. When Ebony hears it, she spins around and runs like a speeding bullet back to where she thinks I am. If she doesn't find me, she immediately starts searching farther along the trail. Occasionally, I hide so well she passes by, and when she gets far enough past me, I yip again. She spins around again and runs right toward me, enjoying every minute. When she catches up, I get a quick kiss right on the lips. She loves this game, as do we.

January 24: The Seizures Have a Pattern

I reviewed the journal today and noticed that, so far, all of Ebony's seizures have been at night or well before dawn—that is to say, when it is dark outside. She always seems stronger during the day. It's curious, and we wonder if this pattern is telling us something about the cause of her epilepsy. Could it have something to do with night? We know that Ebony is developing cataracts. It started two years ago when I spotted a shiny, milky spot in one of her eyes. Before Ebie had seizures, our vet said we should postpone cataract surgery until her cataracts advance. Now we wonder if she'll ever be able to have the surgery.

January 29: Multiple Attacks

I was in Los Angeles on business when Stefan reported that at 6:50 p.m. after he returned from the health club, Ebony had a seizure. As usual, she lost control of her bowels and seized for about a minute. After she recovered, he walked her inside the house for about ten minutes. At 7:10 p.m., he gave her the second Zonisamide. She was restless. Although she watched Stefan preparing his dinner, she didn't eat hers. He went to his office to record the incident. She started barking at him, so he took her outside, but she only stared into the night. Around 8:30, she finally ate her dinner. After taking her out one more time, he took her upstairs and watched news. After walking around for a while she finally fell asleep, but she chose the tight area behind his chair. Around 9:30 p.m., she had another attack. It was short, but recovery took quite some time. Around 11:00 p.m., she finally settled down, and both of them got some sleep.

February 11: More Observations

During the night, Ebie slept in different places upstairs, the final one next to our bed. Stefan got up around 4:20 a.m. to watch the news. Ebie came to the TV room, indicating she wanted to go outside. Stefan took her out. She went over toward the wall where she frequently finds a good spot. She just stood there, and he knew something was coming. Just as they got to the door, she collapsed. The usual followed. Stefan cleaned her up in the first floor bathroom, and then he walked her around in the house.

February 12: 8:15 p.m.

After a good dinner and some playing, Stefan took her out, and as soon as they got close to the stone wall, she sniffed around and started shaking her head– this is now multiple times that her seizures start around the same location. Stefan managed to get her close to the door where she fell, and it happened again.

February 13: 1:00 a.m.

After last night's events, Ebony finally settled down and went to sleep on her bed. Around 1:00 a.m., we woke up hearing a suspicious noise near the sliding door to the balcony. Yes, there she was going into another seizure. We took her into the bathroom to clean her up. It took another hour before she settled down. For the rest of the night, she woke up several times and wanted to walk around. She finally fell asleep toward morning.

February 15: A Good Bath

It has been a bitterly cold winter, but now, it's warming up. Time to give Ebony a bath. As usual, she was well behaved sitting in the tub all soaped up and even staying there alone and not moving while Stefan went upstairs to get a special olive-oil conditioner.

February 20: All Going Well

It has been days since the bath and her fur has remained shiny and fluffy. She looks like a giant woolly caterpillar. We continue to enjoy our walks and she is very attentive. When I get ready for work in the morning, she often stays close, moving with me from room to room. While I'm sitting at my dressing table putting on my makeup, I open a drawer for her so she can sniff the contents. She has always been very curious about the contents of drawers and seems to appreciate that I allow her to investigate them.

February 27: Fourteen-Day Cycle! More Changes

Fourteen days to the day, she had a seizure around 9:00 p.m. last night. Now, it seems to happen when she goes to the window at night to stare out and stumbles when she tries to turn around. Much worse, she had three seizures today at 9:00 p.m., 12:30 a.m., and at 3:00 a.m. All in the dark. What really scares us is how her behavior is changing. She slept much of Monday after the seizures of the previous days and early morning. When I took her for a walk, instead of running and jumping ahead of me, she followed behind very slowly and stopped suddenly. Up ahead, our neighbor was coming with her three dogs, all of whom Ebie has joyfully greeted in the past. This time, Ebie turned around, not wanting to go farther. After a while, we had to head back to the house. I called to Stefan to join us. We went up the hill, but Ebie seemed very unsure of things. She sniffed a lot but appeared to have trouble seeing. One of the maddening things about all of this is not knowing if it is her age, her cataracts, or whatever causing the epilepsy, or all of these combined. You don't know how to treat something you don't understand.

We met with our vet. I printed out my journal and wanted to talk about all the medications I'd read about on the internet and heard about from meeting people. Ebie acted differently when we arrived. Normally, she prances in, breathing with excitement to see who else is there. She usually sits up beside me like a statue, sometimes smirking at the restless dogs in the waiting room. Now, she seemed restless herself. When we got inside the examining room, she didn't jump up on the weight platform as usual. The assistant had to help her up, and she even bumped her head because of being insecure.

Unfortunately, the discussion with our vet didn't shed any new light on matters. He thought all we were experiencing was quite normal for a dog with epilepsy. He said there were other drugs we could try, but he didn't see why we should stop the Zonisamide. He did suggest that we might increase her medication by 50 mg just before we thought the seizure cycle was approaching. He also suggested a tranquilizer that we could give her after a seizure to help her calm down.

March 3: Miracles

I had to make another trip to Los Angeles and toward the end of my one-week stay, Stefan gave Ebie another bath. She loved it and sat down in the water, enjoying the warmth. The reason for this second bath was that we had scheduled Ebie for a haircut. She was wearing heavy winter fur, and we couldn't see her lively eyes. We thought she in turn might have difficulty seeing through her long hair. Ever since she was a puppy, we've taken her to Hindi for a haircut. Although Hindi seems to change salons frequently, we've been able to find and follow her. Ebony is comfortable with Hindi and always gives her a kiss before climbing onto the pedestal. I think Ebony knows that the kiss softens Hindi, and as a result, she is gentle with Ebie and does a beautiful job.

After a haircut, Ebony looks considerably slimmer. We call it the "Ally McBeal" look. She not only looks fantastic but also acts like a completely different dog, in the most positive sense. She leaps and dances around. This time is no different. Ebie is as alert as ever, following us with her eyes and turning her head to listen to whoever is speaking. She's quick in catching her toy no matter how I throw it. Outside, she dodges me, turning quickly on her heels. Her hairpin turns always remind me of the Miata I had when I lived in California. When I come home from work, she dashes up the steps to rough around and play the mind game.

March 10: Rejuvenation

Over the next three weeks, I watched her carefully. Stefan was in L.A. over the third weekend. I was sure something would happen on Sunday night or Monday morning. It was dark at 5:30 a.m., and there was thunder and lightning. Ebie dislikes thunder and lightning, which we referred to as "boom boom." If I say, "Boom boom," she raises her front paw and tries to climb on my lap. However, this time, nothing happened. What's even more surprising is that the jerking or twitching she displays late at night and in the morning is gone. I had the plastic shower curtain draped over the foot of the bed in case she jumped up during the night. She did, but the jerking I had felt in the past is gone.

March 23: Could Emotions Bring on Seizures

Just as I was beginning to feel as if it was all behind us, things changed. Stefan returned Tuesday evening, March 22. I was eager to tell him the good news. Ebie had reversed her symptoms and acts like an eight-year old instead of a dog eleven and a half years old. Her eyes are lively, she cocks her head to catch every word, and there are no more tremors.

Around 2:30 in the morning, Ebie got up and was changing positions when her mouth started twitching and the seizure happened. We got her to the tile-floored bathroom and talked to her until it was over. The only difference this time was that she wasn't as wild afterward as she had been in the past. She was easier to handle and didn't need to be walked around much. After she relaxed, she jumped onto the bed, and all was well for the rest of the night. Could emotions bring on the seizures? Perhaps stimulated by one of us leaving or returning?

The real surprise came the next day. I came home and with daylight saving time, it was still light out at 5:00 p.m. Ebie was very happy to see me and ran up the stairs behind me into our old routine of playing. However, once I'd changed clothes, she seemed somewhat subdued, and perhaps that was a clue. We didn't go through all of our roughing-around procedures: instead, I took her out. She bolted around, happy as a lark, and galloped across the field. I started up the trail path and looked back and saw her with her head up in the air doing something funny with her mouth, and then she was down and paddling.

It was the first time it had happened in the daylight, and I hoped it wasn't the start of a new pattern. We had just been talking about driving out to California in the summer and taking her with us. Now that we were getting used to the routine of her only having them every second week, and until yesterday every third week, we figured we could take her on a trip. We thought we would visit Telluride on the way and spend a few days at the Ice House, where they allow dogs. We dreamed about taking her through town and for walks along the many mountain trails.

Now we're unsure. She still seems alert and strong and just now came up to me while I'm writing—as if nothing is wrong with her health. God, we love her. She's an integral part of our lives. She brings us so much joy, and we talk to her as if she understands every word. Who needs cell phone companionship when you have a pet with such lively eyes wanting to engage you in play and games.

April 9: The Cycle Continues

Approximately two and a half weeks since the last seizure, she had another one at eight in the evening. It was short, and it seemed to take less time to calm her down afterward.

April 10: And Again

It happened when Stefan took her out in the evening. She stood still, mesmerized by something in the distance, and then she fell and had one. It didn't last for very long, and we were able to calm her down. However, at three in the morning, she had another, and this time, it was difficult to calm her down. She was very restless afterward and wanted to walk around a lot. We hesitated to take her outside, and since she had already emptied her bladder during the seizure, we figured she didn't need to do more. She woke up many times during the night, and we got little sleep. Finally, Stefan took her out around 4:00 a.m., and she peed.

The next day, she slept a lot, and then she was herself again: playful, trotting around smiling with her head up. On the trail people admired her as she pranced like a thoroughbred horse showing off. She certainly is a black beauty. The whole thing is very mysterious.

April 24: Fourteen-Day Cycle

I was in California. On Tuesday evening during her usual 8:00 p.m. walk, Stefan told me Ebie had a seizure. It was again a tight spasm and only paddling her legs toward the end.

April 25: Return from California

It was still light at 6:30 p.m. when we thought we would take her for a quick walk. Stefan and I stopped to look at some stones at the side of the path, and when we wanted to move forward, we noticed that she was twitching her mouth, and then it happened.

May 22: Trip to Europe

We're going to Europe, where I'll be attending a philanthropy conference in Portugal, and later we're going to Paris for the World Bank's ABCDE Conference. Stefan joins me on these occasions. The European Foundation Centre Conferences are excellent networking events. Betty has agreed to take care of Ebony. While in Arizona, Betty learned from several people that poodles often have seizures. She feels she can now handle the seizures if Ebony has them. We have explained to her that sometimes Ebie has a cluster of as many as three seizures in a twenty-four-hour period. Betty thinks it will work out. She has emphasized that it was the shock the first time around with the thought that Ebony might be dying that had so upset her when we were in China.

It's been three weeks, and Ebie hasn't had a seizure. In fact, she's been acting fantastic. She is the devilish, alert, black beauty that she is—ready to play, nudging, grinning, eyes sparkling. Then it happened around 1:00 a.m. This time she whimpered and yipped, making short barks while it was happening. We hoped she didn't feel any pain. It took her a while to recover, but she did, and the next day in the afternoon, we took her to Betty's. This was the first trip since China, and we timed it so that we would only be gone one week and a few days.

When we returned from Europe, we learned that Ebie had had three seizures. Betty said most were during the evening walk, and the symptoms were the same. We returned on June 3, and Ebony greeted us with great celebration as always.

June 20: Here We Go Again

After the three seizures, she had while Betty was taking care of her, Ebony seemed fine. Then on June 20 at 7:00 p.m., she had one and another at 11:00 p.m. The next day, she was back to normal.

July 8: More during the Daytime

It has been almost three weeks, and then at 12:45 a.m., Ebie had a seizure in her sleep. It was short. The shock came the next day when she had one at 9:00 a.m. The second one that she has had during daylight. To make it even worse, she also had one at 3:00 in the afternoon while sleeping near my desk. I was working at the computer and heard a loud noise. She must have felt it coming and tried to quickly get up and come toward me when she collapsed. I'd turned by then and saw her struck down, so to speak, as if she'd had a stroke. I felt so bad for her that later when I went shopping, I bought a steak so we could give her a bone that evening.

We had a restless night. She displayed a new bizarre behavior the next day when we went for a walk along the stream. We let her off the leash to get some good sniffs, and then she started turning around and wanted to head back up the trail. We had to put her back on leash to keep her going. It seemed as if she was in her own world, not connecting with us.

July 30: We Passed the Three-Week Mark

Ebie didn't have a seizure yesterday, although it was the third week to the day. She seems to sleep well, sometimes getting up and finding a cooler spot, but not waking us up as much to take her out.

July 31: Purple, Red, and Yellow Pills

All is going well. Ebony jerks occasionally but seems fine. I wonder if the fluctuation might be the medication. We're still administering 50 mg twice a day and an extra 25mg twice a day if we think the cycle is beginning. When we refilled her prescription more than a week ago, it was from a different manufacturer. We discovered that each time we refill, the pills come from whichever manufacturer they have on hand. The first pills were purple, and then came red, and now yellow. Could that make a difference?

I can't imagine what life would be like if we lost her. She radiates such a sweet and powerful energy drawing us into her space. She has a smile on her face as if to say, "I'm here now. Come play with me."

August 11: Five Weeks and She's Fine

Wow, we can't believe it. She's never gone beyond three weeks. She's definitely slower. When we go for a walk, she doesn't keep up with us any longer. She takes all the time in the world, sniffing right and left along the trail.

August 16: California Trip

We're headed to California, and Ebie will be staying with Betty, who happens at this time to have Zeus with her. We worry about going because Ebie is long overdue for a seizure.

August 17: One in Her Sleep

Betty told us Ebie had a seizure in her sleep during the day. She thought Ebie was much more alert after it was all over. We returned August 23 and picked her up. She was ecstatic to see us.

August 31—September 4: Happy Girl

Stefan is in California and I'm alone with Ebie. She is fine so far. We're enjoying each other's company and going on many walks. She has been sleeping solidly throughout the night near our bed. It means I'm able to get some good sleep as well. She seems much more alert: raising her head more often to sniff the air and enticing me with her eyes to follow her. She chased a deer last night and reacts when she sees the fox behind our house. She falls asleep immediately after dinner and it is difficult to wake her up to go upstairs for the night. She loves to be brushed, and as always, she shifts her weight and smiles when I tell her how beautiful she looks. This afternoon after a good brushing, she headed for the front door, thinking it was time to show off her good looks—all with that characteristic smile or laugh that she has had since she was a puppy. The smile disappeared for a while, but it is definitely back and we love to see it.

When I took her for a short walk, the little girl across the street and her mom commented on how pretty Ebie is. With her long ears, soft downy fur, and dark lively eyes, she's indeed a seductress. We could have named her Desiree or Sheba with her stunning features.

September 4: Return Seizure

When Stefan returned, Ebie displayed the usual celebratory greeting, passing through his legs several times to let him know how happy she is. At 2:20 a.m., we awoke to a noise.

Stefan yelled, "She has one." It was a short seizure, and as usual, Ebie lost control. It seemed easier to keep her down immediately following. Stefan walked her around, and then she settled down, and I stroked her until she fell asleep. This morning she was sharp as a tack, cocking her head to interpret what we were saying and barking at me to take her for a walk. When we were on the trail by the brook, we ran into Jean.

When Ebie was a puppy, Jean was someone we met walking her dog, Schultzie, an older schnauzer. Although we meet many people on walks, Ebie immediately singled out Jean as someone special. Ebie could spot Jean a mile away and start pulling on her leash. We always had to hold her down because she wanted to get up on her hind legs and plant some wet kisses on Jean's mouth. Jean seemed to enjoy Ebie's attention since her own dog was now elderly and no longer so affectionate.

The strange thing is that when I encountered Jean last week, Ebie didn't recognize her. Even after Jean stopped and said hello, Ebie didn't make a move. In fact, when Jean reached out to touch her, Ebony pulled away. We may never know if this behavior is a sign of old age, the medication, or some other ailment.

September 25: Another Trip to Europe

We're leaving for Europe, and Ebie hasn't had a seizure since September 4. That means three weeks. We're worried because tomorrow she goes to Betty's and Betty has invited several guests to stay with her for a week. We know Betty loves Ebie and takes good care of her, but we hate to leave her. Ebie is exceptionally attached to us right now. Perhaps there are things going on in her head that we don't know and she's afraid that when we take off, it may be the last time we see each other.

September 30: Emails from Betty Indicate That All Is OK

Ebie is approaching the four-week mark, and nothing has happened so far. It's raining constantly in Arlington, Virginia.

Fortunately, there's sunny weather in Austria. We're enjoying long hikes in the mountains.

One of our favorite walks is along an *alm* (mountain meadow) by the Hochhaderich in Hittisau. The area is large enough to absorb tourists and still provide peace and tranquility. Another favorite is the Dachsbau that twists its way down to the roaring Bolgenach River. A *dachs* is a badger. There are badger tunnels along the way. While we were hiking the area, we met a Dutch couple with two dogs. We stopped to admire the dogs and mentioned how much we had wanted to bring our dog with us. We told the couple that Ebony suffers from seizures and might not take well to being crated and travelling several hours in the hold of a plane.

The couple told us that they had had a dog with epilepsy that died at age thirteen. They ask if we give Ebony water-reduction pills to help reduce the swelling of the brain. We were startled. We'd never heard of treating epilepsy with water-reduction pills. The women told us that, in the end, her dog had come to her and indicated it wanted to be picked up. She was stroking the dog when he went limp and died in her arms.

October 3: The Phone Call

Betty called Stefan's nephew, Eckhard, asking that we call her immediately. We were caught in heavy-back-up traffic because Monday, October 2, was a national holiday in Germany, and hundreds of German tourists were in Austria to enjoy hiking in the mountains. Now they were all on their way back to Germany. When we finally reached a phone and spoke with Betty, we found out that Ebie had had four seizures, and the last one was bad. She had even been unconscious and hadn't moved for a while.

We learned that she had a seizure at 5:18 a.m. on Sunday morning exactly four weeks from the last one. It was short. Then she had another on Sunday afternoon at 3:15 p.m. that lasted longer about two minutes. The third came on Monday morning at 2:45 a.m. She was very confused and agitated afterward. The bad one came at 10:00 a.m. She was out cold after the seizure and didn't respond even after Bob tried to stroke her face.

Betty took her to our vet. Fortunately, they released Ebie later in the day because she seemed OK. Since the vet had given her Valium, Ebony slept over the next day and was very weak, sometimes falling over. We decided to cut our trip short and returned on Thursday. Ebie was happy to see us and, over the next day, got stronger. She even wanted to run outside. However, we noticed that sometimes her hind legs fell out behind her and she'd land on her rump or topple over—her hind muscles were weak.

October 10: Back to a Good Routine

Today is Columbus Day, and Ebony has slept for most of it. She keeps me company as I work at my computer. When I went downstairs for lunch, she remained upstairs. That's why I was thrilled when, around dinnertime, she came down and stood by the back window, looking out. Suddenly, she started barking and began running to the glass door at the other end of the room. Although she slipped on the way when her hind legs gave out, it was great to see her so active and alert. Of course, it was a squirrel.

I told her she was a good girl and clapped my hands in applause. She recognized that I was pleased with her and came prancing toward me. Then she watched us intently as we prepared dinner, waiting to find out whether some of the aromas would find their way into her bowl. We were preparing simmered chicken soup with celery and carrots for her. She gets the soup on top of dry and canned dog food. Hearing the stainless-steel bowl rattle when she gets near the end is always a happy sign. "Boy, was that good."

Later that evening, she brought a toy and tossed it into my lap, which turned into some intensive play. She enjoyed the applause, and later she saw another squirrel and bounced to the window, barking loudly. Since I was still jet-lagged, I went to bed at 7:45 p.m. Ebie went to her bed, but as I began to close my eyes and fall into a light sleep, I felt her jump onto the bed and snuggle close to me. She hadn't done that in a long, long time. I woke around 3:00 a.m. and saw her now sprawled out on the floor. I went over on all fours and put my forehead to hers and listened to her steady breathing, then went back to sleep. It appears that, one week after a seizure, she's back to normal. Sometimes after two weeks, she's OK and then begins to show more signs of restlessness as the cycle repeats itself.

October 11: Adjusting Her Medication

Today, the vet called to check up on her. He ran a test to see whether the Zonisamide levels were within range. The good news is that she's on the low end. Therefore, he again recommended that whenever we go away, we should increase her dosage the week before and during our absence to 75 mg twice a day instead of 50 twice a day. Hope that helps.

We left for California on October 15. Stefan returned October 22. Ebie was fine. Betty thought she was livelier and would jump onto the bed at night. Betty puts plastic and cotton sheets on top of the bed as we do, in case Ebie has a seizure during her sleep.

We learned before our trip that Ebie tested positive again for Lyme disease. We'll be giving her antibiotics for a month. Since Lyme disease can cause swelling of the brain, I'm hoping the antibiotics will help.

October 28: Autumn Leaves

It's sunny and crisp. You can hear the leaves rustling in the wind and feel the cold air tapping your face. Fall always makes me think of the song "Autumn Leaves," which talks about golden days and end of a cycle before winter. My father used to sing "Autumn Leaves," and people remember him for it. When he first came to this country, he earned some money occasionally singing at weddings. When he visited the senior center in his golden days, folks used to say, "Bill, sing us 'Autumn Leaves.'" Today is a golden day, and although Ebie is subdued and doesn't run much any longer, one has to remember she recently turned eighty-four and is already moving toward ninety.

October 29: Snow

From golden days to snow. A nor'easter in October. What a shock. We were supposed to meet friends for dinner, but had to cancel. Just as well. Ebie is going into her fourth week and could be due anytime.

October 30: The Fox

A beautiful, sunny, very crisp day. Ebie enjoyed her walks. We saw a fox ahead on the trail. Because Ebony's eyesight or mental clarity isn't as sharp as it used to be, I had to hold and turn her head in direction of the fox, and then she saw it on her own. She tried to chase it, but she gave up halfway up the hill. She's no longer one of the fastest dogs in the area.

November 1: More Glorious Days

We're surrounded by vivid colors. The bright blue skies are heightened with jet streams. The temperature is in the fifties. Ebie is doing fine, but is very unsteady on her hind legs. She is taking Doxycycline for Lyme disease, and we're giving her pills for her joints.

November 3: Tender Moments

Ebie seems to be moving a little better. Let's see what happens. I looked for her upstairs, and there she was, standing with that bright-eyed, open-mouthed smile. I walked up and pulled her toward my thigh, and standing there, she leaned into me. I held her head close and told her how much we love her. She didn't pull away. She enjoyed every minute.

A closeness she shares with us means so much. Sometimes when she's fully stretched out on the floor, I look into her eyes, while her pupils move back and forth trying to figure out my intentions. Lately, I talk to her about leaving us. I tell her that we'll remember her always or that she should come back to us as another dog. She gives me a strange look when she hears the word "always," perhaps because it isn't yet in her vocabulary or because my tone sounds serious, or maybe both. Right at the punch line, her tongue darts out, and I get a surprise kiss as if she were saying, "Stop that silly talk."

November 5: Shying Away from Friends

I went shopping with Betty. A strange thing happened when we returned. Typically, Ebony is always excited when she sees Betty, but this time Ebie backed away. Our guess is that Ebony may now associate Betty with the emergency clinic and the emergency trip to our vet when we were in California.

November 6: Change the Clocks

We turned the clocks ahead. We were not sure whether to give Ebie her pills at 7:00 as usual or at 6:00, the old 7:00. We decided just to give them to her at the new 7:00. We stopped giving her the extra 25 grams on Friday.

November 7: Seizures Return

At 4:00 a.m. Monday morning, Ebie had a seizure in her sleep. She recovered nicely later that day, and when I came home at 4:30 p.m., she came running and slipped in and out between my legs several times. She even ran up the stairs like old times to play with me in the bedroom. However, later that evening when I was on the phone, Stefan yelled from his office. She had a vicious one and was very restless. Our vet had suggested sometimes giving her a Valium if she doesn't settle down. Therefore, we tried it. She slept solidly until 12:00 a.m. and then got restless again and got up several times. Stefan took her outside twice. Around 4:00 a.m., we got her to quiet down. This morning, I took her for a walk, and she enjoyed sniffing. She was hungry at breakfast.

We think we know the routine now. It's three days after her last seizure, and she is sharp as can be, looking keenly at each of us when we speak to her. She even tried to play with me outside after a walk by dancing in circles, but then she almost fell over—not as limber as we used to be.

November 10: Painful Nail

On Tuesday, Stefan took Ebie for a haircut, which always makes her feel good. Hindi was able to grind some of Ebony's nails, but she noticed that Ebony quickly pulled back her paw when Hindi tried to grind the nail on Ebie's hind foot. Hindi discovered that one nail was broken at the root. Touching it made Ebony flinch, indicating it was painful. Stefan took Ebie to the vet, who said it had to come out right away because it must be hurting her. Fortunately, he was able to do it without anesthesia. It probably hurt like hell, but Ebie came home happy, with a little red bandage around her hind foot. They said she was exceptionally good when they cut the nail and put something on the nerve endings. However, Ebie now gets nervous every time we take her to the vet. She recalls the incident of having her nail removed without anesthesia.

November 17 to 20: Erasing Five Years

Stefan is in L.A., and Ebie has been great. Almost as if, we erased five years. I notice that she seems to be getting stronger and more agile, perhaps because of the Doxycycline or the joint medication pills. Our vet had sold us special pills for joints. Once we finished them, I simply started giving her the Schiff brand we take.

With Stefan gone, I'm even closer to Ebony because normally Stefan and I share the duties of preparing her food, taking her for walks, talking to her and playing. On the first night we were alone, I expected her to go to her bed as usual, but she grinned at me, then leaped like a ballerina onto the bed, and snuggled down near me. I hadn't seen her jump like that all summer, and she did the same the next night and the night after. She looks at me eye to eye and listens very attentively to what I say. Despite the bandage on her hind leg, which I cover with plastic and a rubber band for protection from wet grass, she runs outside and seems very happy.

November 24: Worries as the Year Ends

We do wonder if we're giving her the correct dosage of medication or if there's something else that might be more effective. I've looked on the internet for advice. How much should a dog of Ebony's size and weight receive? Unfortunately, I haven't found clear information. I even posed that question to one of the epilepsy support groups for dogs, but didn't receive a reply.

Recalling the article I had read about a clinical study on triheptanoin, we've been adding coconut oil to Ebie's food and increasing the fat in her diet.

November 26: Living Will

We realized that whenever we go anywhere, we risk the possibility that she might end up in an emergency clinic, if our vet's office is closed. Therefore, we've written a living will for her. Essentially, the living will is written in Ebony's voice, and says she doesn't want to be placed on life support if she remains unconscious from a seizure. We gave a copy to our vet and kept copies to give to anyone taking care of Ebony.

November 27: Ebie Is Doing Well

It is three weeks going on four, and this morning, I saw the signs of the cycle repeating. She seemed dazed, staring straight ahead rather than the usual playful eye movement. However, by the time we went for our walk, she was running up the trail to catch up with Stefan.

December 10: Five-Week Mark

Stefan is in L.A. again. The weather is fantastic—cold and crisp with sunny, clear skies. It reminds me of New Mexico. This Sunday night marks the beginning of the fifth week.

December 11: Then a Cluster of Seizures

They began at 5:00 a.m. and the next day at 2:30 in afternoon. Then again the following morning at 4:00 a.m. and 11:00 a.m.

December 24—28: Another Thankful Christmas and Start of a New Year

Ebony returned to normal again after the attacks in December. It's more than a year since the epilepsy started, and thankfully, Ebie is still with us. We've learned a lot and feel more comfortable with her epilepsy, but it's still mysterious, and there's much we don't know.

We see that Ebony goes through a cycle. As it gets closer to the time of seizures, she begins to act differently. She's restless and insecure, her appetite increases, and she isn't as responsive to us. After the seizures, she's weak. Nevertheless, there's recovery between cycles when she acts like her old self, and we enjoy each other's company. The quality of life for her and for us is good. Although we hate to see her go through a seizure, we prepare for them by placing plastic and cotton sheets on top of all her beds and at the foot of our bed in case she has a seizure when she's sleeping.

Aside from the seizures, she hasn't had an accident in the house and tells us when she has to go out. During the warm weather, we can douche her off outside after a seizure or in the shower in the winter. She's good about being cleaned. For example, she doesn't mind when we clean her feet if it's wet or muddy outside. She always cooperates by patiently letting us wipe one foot at a time before reentering the back door. After we finish cleaning her, she immediately walks extra fast into the house, breathing in and out with excitement as she heads for the kitchen to drink water or check if there's anything left in her bowl. We can see she's slowing down. In September, she turned twelve, the equivalent of eighty-four in dog years.

Invisible deer

"Little mouse"

Snow fun

Happy days along the Potomac

"What's next?"

"Sleeping Beauty"

Characteristic smile along creek trail

YOU CAN'T CONTROL
WHAT YOU DON'T KNOW

January 2012–December 2012

Balancing Act

When we were in China a year ago and spoke by phone with the emergency clinic giving her urgent care, we never thought our sweet Ebony would be with us for another entire year. The vet said Ebony's breathing was labored and she thought our dog was near the end. Therefore, I gave the emergency-clinic vet instructions should Ebony die before we returned home.

Now, looking back, it's been a journey that has caused discomfort and forced us to confront difficult issues. Nevertheless, the three of us are managing, and so far, we have maintained a good balance. We still enjoy quality time together despite the periodic seizures and the mess that they entail, which stresses all of us. We are prepared and exercise common sense about how to handle Ebony's condition, such as placing a plastic sheet or shower curtain over her sleeping areas, then covering the plastic with an old cotton or flannel sheet. If there is an accident, the plastic and sheet can easily be hosed down or thrown into the washing machine. We keep a supply of old towels near her beds to soak up any messes. Because of occasional stiffness in her joints, we bought "memory foam" and cut it to the size of her beds. We learned that it helps to increase her medication before we go away, and occasionally to give her Valium to get her to rest after a seizure. While it's unclear whether it's useful, we're including coconut oil when we feed her in the evening, and we're including more fat as recommended in the ketogenic diet.

Our most useful aid is a harness. I don't know where I got the idea of buying a harness, but now I don't know how we could have managed without it. I found a sturdy one at a local pet store. It runs under Ebony's belly and fits around and between her legs, and it has a firm clasp at the nape of her neck that forms a handle. I chose one in red, which stands out against her dark, curly fur. The usefulness of the harness is that you can grab the clasp instead of her collar to keep her from flopping from side to side. When she comes out of a seizure, Ebony struggles to get onto her feet, but increasingly, her legs have become like rubber, with no strength to hold her up. If we try to prevent her from falling by grabbing her collar, we risk wrenching her neck. The harness provides stability. She actually seems to enjoy wearing it and looks tough, as if she were a service dog ready to pull her weight.

We're getting good at recognizing the cycle and typically will put the harness on her the week before we think she'll have a seizure, and then take it off about a week afterward. It appears that the harness even brings her some comfort because it makes her feel more secure.

We still worry about the medication. Are we giving her a high enough dosage? She's only receiving 100 mg a day (50 mg twice a day) and 150 mg a day before the cycle begins. The emergency clinic had given her 325 mg a day. I've been searching for information on the internet. Although I would never blindly follow medical advice from the internet without also consulting a doctor, from time to time, I've found useful information.

Ebony has been a relatively healthy dog, with one exception. When she was about eight years old, the claws or nails on her paws began to split right down the middle, close to the quick. It began with one nail. She held up her paw to us, and when we examined it, we found a split nail that looked like the beak of a bird. We took her to our vet, who said the nail needed to be removed. Ebony was given anesthesia. It was a simple procedure. To protect Ebie's paw, the vet's assistant put a red adhesive bandage around it that looked like a sock. Ebony loved to show the sock to people. I remember the first time Betty came after the surgery. Ebony went to the front door and sat like a statue, and when I opened the door for Betty, Ebony extended the paw with the red sock so Betty would see it immediately. Betty just melted.

Sadly, two weeks after the surgery, we found another claw split down to the quick and saw others that were starting to split. Our vet said he was sure what was causing the split claws, but wanted to send a tissue sample to the lab. Ebony underwent another minor surgery with anesthesia. Before we even got the lab results, I began searching the internet and found an article about research being done at Cornell University on a disorder found in large dogs called symmetrical lupoid onychodystrophy (SLO), an autoimmune disease, which can cause severe claw problems in otherwise apparently healthy dogs. It is characterized by the loss of claws from more than one paw and can result in lameness. The treatment suggested in the Cornell study article was large dosages of Omega 3 oil. I wrote to the doctor who conducted the study, who pointed me to additional articles and treatments for SLO. When Ebony's lab results came back, our vet called to say she has SLO and that we should treat her with Omega 3. He was surprised when I mentioned that I was corresponding with the doctor at Cornell who's widely recognized for the initial study.

I turned to Cornell again to try to determine how much seizure medication a dog of Ebony's size and weight should receive, but didn't receive an answer this time. None of the blogs and chat rooms about dogs provided enough detail on dosage.

January 5: Slowing Down

The early-morning sky is a lilac color with wisps of orange and red and patches of icy blue. It forms a stunning backdrop to the stark outline of the trees. When the sun finally shows itself, it is frosty white, reminding us that it's winter and the barren earth around us is in a state of sleep. The moment recalls the Greek myth of Persephone and the changes of the seasons. When Persephone had to retreat to the underworld, life above slowly faded away and went into a state of sleep until she returned in the spring. I loved myths as a child and had once narrated and set to music the story of Persephone for a speech class.

Ebony is doing fine. She has slowed down significantly, though it's unclear whether this is from the medicine or her age. She's now twelve and a half. During our walks, she follows me faithfully as she did when she was a puppy. If I stop, she stops and looks around, sometimes sniffing the spoor of deer or fox. She no longer dances around me or dashes ahead up the hill. But she's still with us and we love having her.

Today when I stopped on the trail, she approached panting and smiling. She lifted her head as if to say, "Come on, give me a smile back." I did and then gave her a pat and said, "Good girl." I think Ebony knows we're trying to take good care of her. After all, she picked us out when we were looking at her sisters and brothers. She probably analyzed us immediately and knew that if we didn't give her what she needed, she would be able to train us.

January 11: A Cluster of Them

I left for L.A., and Ebie had a series of five seizures that ended the afternoon of the next day. We hope these clusters of several seizures within a twenty-four-hour period are not a new norm.

When I spoke with Stefan a day later via Skype, Ebony had already recovered and was resting near him on the bed in his office. Quite often on these Skype talks, I hear Ebony shake her head, causing the tags on her collar to jingle. The sound is so clear that I get shivers because, in that instant, I think she's with me in California. Sometimes, Stefan places his headset over Ebie's ears and I talk to her. She seems to listen intensely. Even when she stays with Betty, we sometimes talk to her by phone. Betty says Ebony comes trotting into the room when the phone rings, sits, and looks up at her. If we are on the other end, Betty puts the receiver by Ebony's ear. Hearing our voice seems to have a calming effect on her.

February 2: Wanting Her Head Rubbed

Last night Ebony jumped onto the bed and immediately snuggled with her head against my chest. I kept rubbing. If I stopped, she would push her head even harder against me, telling me she wanted more. For a moment, I thought about the Dutch couple we'd met while hiking in Austria. The wife had said that near the end their dog had leaned against her leg. She'd picked her dog up and patted him with long strokes, and then suddenly, she felt him go limp in her arms.

February 15: Five-Week Clusters

I felt the bed shaking and bolted up to see Ebony's mouth twisting and her feet frantically paddling in the air. Stefan was in L.A. I got her off the bed onto the floor. She started twisting urgently to regain her composure. I managed to get her legs into her harness while she flopped from side to side. She wanted to stand but wobbled and collapsed. Her legs were useless, like those of a scarecrow. She continued to flop, wide eyed and panting heavily, with her tongue hanging to one side.

Then as she gained some strength and got on her feet, she pulled me as she desperately tried to walk it off. We surged through the upstairs rooms, around and around, bedroom, hall, TV room, bathroom, and back again, repeating the pattern at least ten times. It was exhausting just trying to keep a hand on the harness while she pulled me forward with incredible strength. Finally, I was able to get her down the stairs by gripping the harness and pulling up so that her legs floated on the steps. I got her into Stefan's office, where she finally collapsed on her office bed.

Now she was ready to rest for a short while. I knew I should stay close to watch her. Poor little girl would repeatedly try to get up and walk. I didn't want to risk a broken leg if she slipped on the hardwood floor. She had no sense of balance. So I turned on Stefan's computer, and although the air in the room was icy cold, I started looking through my emails. She was breathing heavily. I could see her diaphragm heave like a wave with each deep breath. It was now close to 7:00 a.m. EST, and I knew Stefan would already be awake. Therefore, I called to tell him the news.

It was five weeks to the day. She had another seizure at 2:00 in the afternoon, at 12:00 a.m. Sunday morning and 5:00 a.m. on Monday morning. A new pattern with more clusters over a period of days seemed to be forming.

February 18: Back to Normal

Over the next few weeks, Ebony seemed fine. She roamed the house, finding comfortable places to rest. When Ebony was a young dog, we noticed that throughout the day she followed the movement of the sun by changing locations. She chose the upstairs TV room to catch the morning sun and an hour later a section of our bedroom as the sun moved toward the west. In the afternoon, she enjoyed the warmth of the sun coming through the living room window as it warmed the area of the small sofa.

She still seems to like keeping an eye on what we're doing. She comes to visit me from time to time as I compose on my computer. Not knowing how long she'll be with us, I always stop and welcome her as she approaches with that grin on her face. She still enjoys the head rub. Now I notice that when I rub her head hard, her left front leg automatically starts to slide from under her. It's a reflex, but I wonder if it's connected to a brain disorder.

February 21: She Doesn't Gain Weight

Ebony's appetite is exceptionally hearty. We wonder why she does not gain weight, given all she eats. We continue cooking fresh soup and adding it to other food. Over the past two years, there have been nationwide concerns about dog food. Much to the surprise of many pet owners, we've discovered that some of the well-known manufactures of dog food import portions of the ingredients from China. According to the alerts and recalls on the news, the imported ingredients have caused illness and even the death of some dogs. In addition to the food we prepare for her, we spoil her by sharing some of our food while we're eating at the dining room table. She sits perfectly erect like a statue while we eat. When we're almost finished, she begins to shift her position, eagerly awaiting her turn. She's exceptionally gentle when she takes the food. I love the tickle of the soft fur around her nose and her warm breath as she makes sure she's getting every final crumb. Some people would disapprove of all this attention we give her. But she's part of the family, and we love her.

March 1: Awakening of Spring

We've begun to notice the first signs of spring with the increase in the twittering from the birds that begins around 5:15 in the morning. There are always certain birdcalls within the morning chatter that one hears only when it's spring. The ground is still hard, but little blades have pushed their way through the soil, and although the trees are still barren, one can see green beginning to appear along the branches and tree trunks. The earth is waking up.

March 15: Upping and Lowering the Medication and Coconut Oil

For some time now, we've been increasing Ebony's medication several days before we think the cycle will start. Instead of 50 mg twice a day, we give her 75, for a total of 150 instead of 100. We also are still adding coconut oil to her food. I found some good coconut-oil products at Whole Foods. When I asked one of the store associates where to find it, she mentioned that several people who have epilepsy had asked for it.

Once we lower the medication after the cycle, she perks up a bit and is more active and alert. She appears more comfortable and therefore more attentive to what we do and say to her. Although she appears hard of hearing, she watches us intently. Yesterday, she paid me a visit in my office. I looked directly into her eyes, and she responded by moving her eyeball from left to right as if asking, "What's up?" I even received a quick kiss on the chin.

However, we have observed that her hips seem to be stiff and she sometimes acts lame. She's still able to jump onto the small sofa but not onto our bed or into the back seat of our car. Therefore, we've started a new routine. She first places her front paws up on the bed or seat of the car. Then she waits for us to push her so she can scramble up the rest of the way. Sometimes, we're delayed and then she looks at us as if to say, "Hey, I'm waiting."

March 18: She Passed the Five-Week Mark

Outside, spring is dressed in full glory with flowering almond to be followed by cherry blossoms and then an explosion of flowering azaleas. Even the morning light feels different as it filters through the trees.

It has been five weeks, and for the last two, she has been on extra medication. She's chosen to settle down in the middle room where she can keep an eye in all directions, including the front door. She is much quieter and her eyesight has gotten worse. Both eyes have milky areas. When a visitor or one of us comes to the front door, she has to sniff carefully to figure out how to act. When she recognizes our scent, she bows her head in a submissive gesture, indicating she's glad. But she no longer rushes through our legs and displays excitement.

She's still attentive. Sometimes when I pass by her in the middle room, she lifts her head and stares at me dead on, drawing me in. We both check on each other in a reassuring way, signaling that all is OK. I find myself telling her again and again what a good girl she is and that she is a very pretty and a smart doggie. She's still with us even if the routine is changing. I'm touched that she still climbs the stairs to visit me in my study, but now she seldom remains with me.

March 21: Fox Encounter

A few days ago, Stefan was walking Ebony toward dusk and spotted a fox. It did not run away; instead, the fox cowered and watched them pass. Perhaps the fox could sense that Ebony's no longer a threat or (even worse) that she's weak. Just two years ago, Ebony would have charged like a bouncing kangaroo. We realize that we should always be near Ebony now when she's outside at dusk. I would not be surprised if the fox tried to get at her. We remember the stories we heard when we lived in California with Brookie and Windy. Coyotes are known to go after small dogs and cats. While Ebony is anything but small, her state of weakness could attract the fox.

April 3: We Lost Zeus

Betty called with the sad news. Zeus was Ebony's closest friend. Betty told us that on one occasion during a seizure, Zeus bent down and licked Ebony's face. In better times, they played well together and sometimes imitated each other's habits. Zeus had a sore on his leg that didn't heal. They were in Arizona for the winter. They took him to several vets, and for a while, he received cortisone shots. However, the tumor kept coming back and obviously hurt him because he couldn't put weight on that leg. Finally, they took him to a vet who informed them that Zeus had an even more serious condition—a very weak heart. They made the difficult decision to put him to sleep. Before he received the injection, they told him repeatedly how much they loved him. They felt he knew what they were trying to convey. Our pets know.

May 2: Premature Heat

The visual poetry of the awakening of the earth in spring with displays of delicate white-and-pink blossoms and crisp tulips pushing through the ground has turned into the Amazon. It rains each week, and muddy water runs down the side of the road by the water tower. Everything green has tripled in size. The vegetation almost touches the house and is so dense that I sometimes think an intruder could kidnap us and no one would hear our cries for help.

May 15: Distant and in Her Own World

Ebie is very quiet and noticeably less affectionate. If I bend down and look her in the eye, she doesn't return the look or give me a kiss. To an outsider, she still looks like a princess, elegant and poised. But when I lie down beside her, she turns her head away. Is she preparing us?

She appears more and more to be in her own world. She looks at us when we talk to her, but if she's in another room and we call, she often doesn't respond. She still comes to visit me when I'm working at my computer in my office upstairs. I continue to acknowledge her when I hear her coming by turning in my chair and calling out to her "Hello, Ebie." I pat my leg now to give her a sign in case her hearing is bad. However, she only comes halfway toward me, her toenails tapping on the wooden floor, and then she turns and retreats to the landing on top of the stairs. She settles down on the bed we placed there for her.

Ebie roams the house more than before. Instead of greeting us when we come home, we find her either upstairs at the top of the steps, in the upstairs TV room, or on her bed in our bedroom. She looks fantastic. People still think she's eight years old or younger. She's slim despite her hearty appetite. Her short haircut emphasizes her long, elegant nose and her long, soft, curly ears. When she sits stretched out, her profile is irresistible, and I have to get closer and give her a hug. However, in the past when I hugged her, I would get a kiss in return. Now when I circle her with my arms, she just stares straight ahead. Is she distancing herself for a reason? What goes on in that head of hers?

June 19: Difficulty Climbing Steps

Ebie continues to act independently and roams the house despite obvious arthritis. Recently, Stefan went to L.A., and it was nearing Ebony's cycle. Her hind legs would shake as if she was frightened, but it was her muscles that were failing. She tries to climb the steps but has to stop often to keep from slipping. When she is unsure of her footing, she turns to head back down and then slips and tumbles to the bottom. If I am upstairs and hear her climbing with repeated stops, I run to help her before she turns and tumbles. On a few occasions, I've been too late and witnessed her fall to the bottom of the steps. The incident appears to hurt me more than her. I always run down to embrace and cuddle her. However, she gets up, breathes in and out, and just wants to move on.

June 15: First Seizure since February

Instead of five weeks apart, it came at 4:30 p.m. after five months! It was relatively short, but she was very upset for more than an hour afterward. Stefan took her outside. The weather was pleasant: dry heat with a light breeze. Ebony tried to walk in the grass but kept tipping over. He got her to lie down and just rest. They sat for a while, and every so often, she tried again to move. She was panting rapidly and seemed anxious. Stefan gave her a sedative that our vet had prescribed. That evening, Stefan decided to continue giving her the extra dosage of her medication (he had stopped that morning). She was fine over the next few days.

Now back to her normal dosage, she walks better and smiles more. She is also more responsive to conversations and the mention of her name. We find her all over the house—after all, it is her home too.

July 2: Clever Girl

It's 97, but with the humidity, it feels more like 105. The air conditioning is running continuously. You cannot go outside without feeling as if the sun is pointing at you wherever you go. I obtain some comfort by looking at the hydrangea arranged in a cobalt-blue vase. The brilliant blue of the blossoms and the generous green leaves have a cleansing and energizing affect. Ebie is stretched out, gone to the world. She sleeps peacefully most of the day.

Much to our surprise, Ebony has adapted to going up the oak steps. We marvel at how smart she is. One hind leg is worse than the other. She knows that if she tries to use two feet at a time she may start sliding. Since she cannot just leap up the stairs as before, she therefore takes one step and foot at a time. First, she places the good front leg on the next step, then the other front leg. Then she places the firmer hind leg on the lower step and only then brings up the weak hind leg. She repeats the pattern until she reaches the top. Watching her reminds me of a person trying to climb steps with a heavy cast on one leg.

We've had visitors from Europe for several weeks. They love Ebie, and she allows them to hold her. Hugging Ebony is like hugging a bear. She's a big girl.

As the hot summer lingers on, we're careful not to overexpose Ebony to the heat. The other day while at a gas station, we saw a person pulling a little puppy by a leash across the hot concrete. I guess it didn't occur to him that walking on concrete that has been heating up in the sun all day might be uncomfortable and burn the bottom of the puppy's feet despite the padding dogs have under their paws. I wish I could make the owner take off his shoes and socks and try it.

August: Hot Hot Hot

The humidity is suffocating, and the air is loud with the sound of insects. Due to the high heat, most of the flowers wilted away. Only riots of ever-strong black-eyed Susan (Rudbeckia hirta) with their bright and bold yellow-orange petals have survived, running up and down the hillside of our house.

August 2: Clusters and Frighteningly Weak

Ebie surprised us with a seizure, and four more followed over the next day. The night before she had an eating frenzy and even nervously crunched the ice we had in her bowl of water. Following the seizure episodes, she was much weaker than we've ever seen her. She wobbles and falls over even now. She even fell into the wall while trying to bend to drink water from her bowl. To help, we hold the bowl for her. Her jerks are large, shaking her entire body as opposed to just her head. She's so weak that we're worried the end is coming, and we're making more of an effort to tell her how good she is and that we will always love her.

August 10: Stronger Than Ever

It's more than a week, and she has fully recovered. Even her hips that have become a chronic problem seem better, and now she sets out at the bottom of the steps and thrusts herself up without stopping at each step. In the morning, she's almost ready to jump onto the bed, but still needs a lift. She has started using her paw again to indicate "more" (another cookie, more scratching of the head), and she even approaches when I crook with my finger. Last night, she placed her head on my chest so she could receive lots of head stroking. Outside, she runs again in small bursts and chases her tail at night. We stopped the second pill four days after the last seizure, and doing so always makes a difference. Nevertheless, this time the difference is huge. Wish we knew why.

Although she sleeps away most the day, choosing to be near one of us, she comes alive when we sit together and after meals. She still spots and responds to the fox though her bark is now hoarse and sounds like kennel cough. She listens and acknowledges commands, and aside from losing control of her bowels during a seizure, she's never had an accident in the house.

September 2: Eucalyptus and Lavender

Our visitors have left, and Ebony is still doing great. Today, we gave her a bath, and she enjoyed it. We always use Johnson & Johnson baby shampoo so the soap will not burn her eyes. Before rinsing, we use eucalyptus and sometimes lavender shower gel. It leaves a nice aroma for several days, which I notice when I bury my face in her fur.

October 2: Harvest Moon

The trees burn bright orange and blood red. The trail by the water tower is paved with chestnuts and acorns. If not careful walking over them, one might start to roll and slide down the hill. Ebony is enjoying her walks, and we're happy she's doing so well. We even think we may be able to drive to California for Christmas, bringing her with us. She has done so well since the seizure clusters in August.

October 16: Vaccinations

Today, Ebony is due for her blood work and her annual physical. Our vet also thinks we're all doing well. I keep emphasizing that the seizures have a pattern. I have been reading about hormonal causes and wonder if Ebony's pattern is a result. Our vet says her blood work hasn't indicated the need for hormonal testing. She's due for a series of shots, but knowing that shots sometimes contribute to a seizure, he recommends giving Ebony only the rabies shot.

October 17–20: The Worst So Far

The only good news is that it has been more than twelve weeks and no seizures. Now she's had a cluster of nine: October 17, 2.45 p.m. and 8:15 p.m; October 18, 3:15 a.m., 9:35 a.m., 3:14 p.m., and 9:30 p.m.; and October 19, 3:15 a.m., 9:10 a.m., and 1:15 p.m. For three days, she has had difficulty standing without tipping over. She can't make it up the stairs without help. It's difficult to clean her because she's so weak. I hold her water and food bowls up close, and she eagerly wolfs down everything. In fact, she isn't really herself now when she eats after a cluster of seizures: she seems to forget not to bite down on our fingers or hand. She's reverting to her feral roots.

Since she had gained a little strength, we took her outside today and were happy to see her follow us. Her smile is back, but she fell over many times as we tried to walk the trail. She can't yet crouch to pass her urine. Her poop just falls out in the back in little balls. After two days of this, we decided to give her a bath. We were careful to make sure we dried her well. She seemed to enjoy the warmth.

We don't know if the rabies shot triggered the cluster. I read that the State of California is trying to get shots waived if a dog is suffering from seizures and other illnesses. We called our vet. He didn't want to discuss it and said, "See a neurologist." I began asking neighbors for recommendations.

October 29: Recovery and Urinary Tract Infection

I left for Cyprus to chair a panel on innovative technology for protecting cultural property from looting and theft. I was worried that Stefan would have to face taking her to the vet to put her to sleep without me. But she got better. She got better. Moreover, while she could not go up the stairs before I left, it was great news when I talked to Stefan from Cyprus and learned that she was marching up the steps again. When I returned, she seemed normal again in every way. However, a few days later she became nervous and had to constantly pee outside, and then she started to pee inside the house. This is Ebony, an exceptionally clean dog who, aside from her seizures when she loses control, has never had an accident in the house.

I noticed some milky substance coming out of her vagina and putting two and two together suspected she had a urinary tract infection. We took her to our vet and reminded him that in October she'd had ten seizures and that this time it took her several difficult days to recover until she was back to normal. He shook his head and said, "She's the miracle dog." He prescribed antibiotics, and I asked if I could give her cranberry pills as well. He said, "Yes." She got over the urinary tract infection, and we were very glad with the holidays approaching that she was back to "normal."

November 2: Sheets of Rain Drumming on the Skylights

The colors of the remaining fall leaves jump out in the wetness. Ebie is nestled on the bed at the top of the stairs where she can watch the front door and keep an eye on me as I sit in front of the computer. She's curled up like a woolly ball but lifts a sleepy head whenever I move by her. I can't resist giving her a hug. Her velvety skin feels so good, especially after a recent haircut. What a knockout she is. So elegant with her long legs and nose. Thankfully, she's fine, and we're enjoying our time together.

Holidays

Thanksgiving and Christmas came and went. We often decline invitations to go places because we don't want to leave Ebony alone for too long. Neighbors who were renovating a house in the Pennsylvania countryside invited us for Thanksgiving dinner, but we declined when they said we couldn't bring Ebony. Since it was a four-hour-plus drive each way, we just felt it was too long a time to leave her alone. Betty was in Arizona for the winter.

Over the holidays, we had guests, reunions with family members, great food and wine. Ebie hasn't been interested in toys for the past two years, so I no longer buy them and wrap them up at Christmas. Some things change whether you want them to or not.

Holding a bone for her

Protective sock after foot surgery

Showing off her haircut near Harper's Ferry

A WILL TO LIVE

January 2013—September 30, 2013

Our Poor Little Girl

B arren trees carve sharp silhouettes against the cold, blue sky. The only motion in the chilly air is the frantic twitching of a few shriveled oak leaves.

At Thanksgiving, we entered year three of living with Ebony's epilepsy. We're thankful that Ebony is still with us. Sadly, however, her side effects and suffering have increased. The change from periodic seizures to large clusters over a forty-eight-hour period is having a bad effect.

More than once, Ebie has appeared close to the end. She couldn't help herself and didn't even seem to recognize us. We've nursed Ebie back while being unsure whether she'll ever return to normal: whatever "normal" means, given her condition and age. After a few days, she improves and manages again. She displays tremendous strength in how she struggles to recover each time. We admire her determination. Nevertheless, the increase in the number of seizures over a period of a few days is taking its toll. In particular, she's getting much weaker mentally. Each cluster seems to whittle away her spirit. We feel as if we're losing her. After the ten seizures that occurred over the course of two days in October, we've begun to discuss what would constitute an end and how to handle it.

The situation is quite different from what we experienced with Brookie and Windy. Brookie, the mother, and Windy, her puppy, both reached age thirteen. As each became ill in their senior years, when their time came, we took them to our vet to put them to sleep. We stood by as he administered the shot. In the case of our sweet little ones, they'd stopped eating and slept most of the day; minds as well as bodies were shutting down, telling us it was time. Ebony, however, is still strong physically and is functioning, even if in her own world. She indicates a will to live.

It would be difficult for us to take Ebony to our vet to put her to sleep. She's developed a dislike for that office, dating back to the removal of her broken claw without anesthesia. We don't want to risk her being upset at such a heartbreaking time. People we meet have shared their stories, and, in several cases, we learned that their vet came to their home when the time came to put their pet to sleep. We inquired with our vet, but he said that his office no longer performs that service. Therefore, we were grateful soon after when a neighbor mentioned that she knew of a vet who would come to a house to administer the injection. She also said that the vet owned a standard poodle. I made an appointment and introduced the doctor to Ebony.

When I brought Ebony into the office, the staff took note and commented on her regal and stunning looks. Ebony smiled as she entered, loving the attention, as if she knew they were struck by her beauty. I explained to the vet that Ebony was now thirteen and suffered from epilepsy. I mentioned that the seizures were weakening her and coming in clusters of eight to ten over two to three days. She nodded with understanding and said she would be willing to come to our house at the appropriate time. It was a great relief to have a plan when and if we needed it.

February 4: Ebony's Diet and Administering Her Medication

It's exceptionally cold outside. Ebony's OK. She's a miracle dog, as our vet says. She just doesn't give up. As bad as it's been, she fits right in again, such as sitting between us at breakfast eating out of her bowl while we have our cereal. She keenly watches every move we make and still gets nervous when there's barely anything left on our plates because she's expecting us to give her leftovers.

We've continued to increase the fat in her diet, sometimes preparing chopped meat or sausage, which we mix with some canned food and generously douse with homemade soup, from either beef neck bones or chicken. There are carrots and celery in the soup, and she gets some vegetables as well as some of the meat.

She is very good about taking her medication. She always sits nicely and lets us lift her chin, open her mouth, and then insert the pill far back on her tongue. She stares directly at us with wide eyes until the pill is gone. I feel that we have her total trust. We often wrap the pill in some peanut butter or, at night, some chopped meat. I tell her what the pill is for, although I doubt she understands. It's a habit that dates back to my mother's cancer. One of her doctors urged her to envision how the different medications she was taking worked together to fight the cancer.

We've gotten used to Ebony's jerks and twitching. One thing new we're noticing is that she seems to get confused from time to time and crosses her front legs awkwardly as if the signals in her head were misfiring and she's uncoordinated.

February 9: Bitter Wind Overnight

How lucky we are that the nor'easter has passed over us. New York and New England were not as lucky. It's almost strange that we haven't had any snow this winter. Four years ago, at one point, it snowed for five days, and after shoveling, more fell. The snow got so high that, when Stefan dug a trench behind the house for Ebie to go out, it ended up being more than two feet high. It began a foot from the back door, made a sharp left, and ran up the hill straight to the bird feeder. When it was finished, we opened the back door, and just as Ebie was ready to leap out, she had to stop short in order not to hit the wall of snow. She appeared shocked, as if asking, "What kind of trick are you playing?"

February 12: Stinky Foot

Today, we took Ebony on our daily walk up the trail by the water tower. Leaves and sticks covered the ground. Still no snow. A few days later, we noticed that Ebony was having trouble with her left hind paw. Sometimes she shakes it, and she is noticeably lame. We tried to inspect it, but she is very uncomfortable when we take the foot in our hands. We noticed a fungal smell.

From time to time, Ebony has minor ailments. We try not to get alarmed and, whenever possible, apply common sense. Now, looking at Ebie's sore foot and noticing its bad odor, we thought we saw something like a growth between the claws. If we try to touch it, she immediately pulls her foot back. We made some chamomile tea and soaked a sterile cotton pad with it, and then taped the pad to her foot. She didn't like it at first, but then let it be and slept. When we removed the pad in the morning, we saw that what had looked like a wart was a twig-like seedpod that was so tightly wedged into Ebie's paw that it looked like it was growing out of her foot. Since it was moist from the chamomile, we pulled it out, and then soaked her foot some more. Over the next few days, the lameness was gone.

March 4: Can it Get Any Worse

It began after Stefan left for California. I went to work, and, since we were unsure when she might have a seizure, I decided to confine her to Stefan's office. We don't have a basement. The space contains one of her beds, and it's near a large floor-to-ceiling window so she can look out easily. She seemed fine. Whenever one of us leaves, the other always feels closer to Ebony. We know she depends on us, and that always draws us closer to her.

I came home early because I wanted to make sure she was OK. When I opened the door to the office, I saw dirt on the floor and puddles of urine and poop smeared in several places. It must have been a violent attack, and, in the process, Ebony had tipped over the large potted plant in the corner. Now she was resting quietly, reclining like a princess, watching for my reaction to the mess. I felt sorry for her and went over to comfort her. It wouldn't make sense to scold her. She cannot control the seizures and the loss of bowel control that are part of the process. She was happy to see me. I noticed that she had poop caked to her fur. I took her outside and let her roam while I went back to clean up the mess.

This had been Ebie's first seizure since October. Five months! I removed her bed, which was soaked with urine, and the rug under Stefan's desk. I could throw her bed with the plastic sheet and towel into the wash. The rug had to be discarded. We'd learned to use white vinegar mixed with a little water to clean the wooden floor in the office. The solution kills the urine odor, especially if urine gets between the cracks of floorboards; it also helps prevent the wood from darkening.

The phone rang while I was cleaning. It was Stefan. He was shocked when I told him. He lamented that it had happened when he was away. Our worry, given her change from isolated seizures to clusters over a period of days, was that there might be more to come. I had stopped giving her the extra 25 mg of Zonisamide that morning. Now, we decided I should keep giving it to her. I also knew I should stay home for the next few days.

Sure enough, at 4:00 p.m., she had another one—as usual, feet kicking in the air and urine pulsing. When it ended, the heavy, wrenching coughs started. Then she immediately wanted to stand, but had trouble and slipped on the wooden floor.

I had difficulty keeping her calm because she was compulsive about wanting to walk. In trying to hold her back, I was amazed at her strength. I opened the door and led her by her collar throughout the house. I was exhausted long before she got tired and settled down again.

When she finally rested, I gathered all the dirty towels, plastic, and bed and quickly took them upstairs and tossed them into the washing machine. I got her harness and went back down. Then, I got her dinner ready. Since she was weak, I held her water and food bowl while she ate. She sniffed the food as if she did not know what it was, and then devoured it eagerly.

At 8:30 p.m., she had another attack. Same routine. She was very confused and wanted to surge through the house as if she were trying to escape from whatever had taken control of her. I decided I'd better sleep downstairs in the guest room, which is near Stefan's office.

At 3:00 a.m. on Tuesday morning, she had another seizure. I'm a very light sleeper and woke up immediately when I heard something. What particularly worried me was how she began whining afterward and came toward me, pushing her face into my chest as if she were trying to hide there. I felt useless not knowing how to make it better for her. After I was able to quiet her down and give her a tranquilizer, I decided it was best if I moved one of her clean beds into the guest room where I was sleeping. I placed it on the tile floor in front of the bathroom. We didn't get to sleep until 4:30 a.m., and then at 6:00 a.m., I woke because she was having another one. At 9:00 a.m. came number six. I thought it best to increase her medication, yet again, to 100 mg twice a day until she recovered.

By now, there were several dirty towels and plastic sheets soaked in urine and poop, including the covers of her soiled beds. I placed the dirty things outside and let her roam there while I cleaned up. The weather forecast indicated the possibility of snow.

Poor little girl had another seizure at 1:00 p.m., and then another at 4:30 p.m. I was thankful that I'd remained home.

Ebony was getting very weak and unstable. She kept falling into the wall or being knocked off her feet each time she tried to stand. At one point, she fell hard on the floor and her tooth cut her tongue. My greatest fear now was how I would handle getting her to the vet if she broke a leg. I tried to place large sheets of tarp on the wooden floor to help her gain some traction. We went to bed at 8:00 p.m.

I was exhausted and felt I hardly had time to eat because if she wanted to move, I had to watch to make sure she did not fall. At 10:00 p.m., she had another. When we finally fell to sleep at 11:30 p.m., it didn't take long until she had yet another at 1:00 a.m. At one point, she tried to get up and come to the side of my bed. I immediately woke, but she moved too fast and fell into the night table by my bed, causing a glass with water to smash on the floor. I jumped out of bed to sweep up the broken glass before she stepped on it. Her compulsion to move and walk was almost as if she were possessed.

On Wednesday morning, we woke to snow falling outside. So far, she'd had ten seizures, and I thought it was all over. I decided to think of it as a new day and, with the snow outside, make a hearty breakfast with eggs and sausage that Ebony could share with me. I left the guest room door open and was getting breakfast ready when Ebony came padding toward me like a big, woolly bear. No doubt, the sausage sizzling in the pan had roused her curiosity. She was smiling, although wobbly on her feet. It warmed my heart to see her. As she entered the kitchen and lifted her head to catch the aroma, she suddenly fell, and on came seizure number eleven.

What was particularly agonizing was that, unlike other times when she appeared to be in pain and would look me straight in the eye and whine or bark, (sometimes even pushing her head into my chest), with her vocal cords now muffled, the bark came out hoarse. The information about seizures on the internet describes whining and barking just like what we were experiencing. However, it was heart-wrenching to think she might be feeling pain, and, in my mind, I felt we had to consider her welfare.

Throughout all this, I would talk to Stefan via Skype. He was shocked that she was having so many seizures. Stefan was in California because the bathroom in our condominium was being demolished. He was to return on Monday, and I was to leave on Tuesday to oversee the next stage of the project, the tile and grout work. Fortunately, he used miles to obtain his ticket.

Not being able to sleep at night because of Ebie's compulsive need to move about, I asked him to come back early and help me with her so I could get some rest before getting on the plane myself. That day, Ebie had more seizures. When it was all over, she'd had fifteen! The washing machine was constantly in use. It helped to be able to first place the dirty items outside, despite the freezing conditions, and lay down fresh towels and plastic.

Before Stefan returned on Saturday, I felt I had to give Ebie a bath. It was difficult because she was limp and weighs about sixty-five pounds. As I soaped her with eucalyptus shower gel, she started to sink beneath the water. The harness was off, so I had to heave her up several times. She reacted a little better after she was dry. She must have felt good after getting rid of the urine and poop that had been stuck to her fur. As I was drying her with the towel, I kept telling her what a good girl she was, and that she was such a pretty and smart doggie.

When Stefan arrived, he was shocked to see Ebie so weak. He spoke to her softly and tried taking her out, but she constantly fell over. We could not take her upstairs to the bedroom, so we left her in Stefan's office.

March 11: Los Angeles

Ebie's increase in seizure clusters over the past several months made it impossible for us to travel together. It would have been much easier for both of us to be in L.A. when we were interviewing contractors and making decisions on tile and bathroom fixtures. We did not want to leave her at the vet. Brookie's life went downhill after she received a heavy dosage of medication when she had a seizure while boarding at the vet. We felt that Ebony had become too much for Betty to handle.

I left for L.A. feeling sad about the road ahead. Miraculously, she pulled through yet again. When Stefan told me she was able to go up the stairs to the bedroom, I was happy on the one hand, but at the same time, I had to ask myself how long this could go on. We don't want it to get worse for her than it is now.

One of the nicest pastimes while in L.A. is hiking and walking the side streets in an area like Pacific Palisades. There are hills running along the ocean and streets that twist and turn named after places on the Amalfi Coast. Some of the houses are modern structures hanging on the side of a cliff, and others are Spanish-style. A few are known by the names of celebrities who once live there, like the Joseph Cotten and Thelma Todd houses. Almost every morning, the California sun rises to cast its radiance over the ocean for another beautiful day.

Today, I walked up Castellamare Drive while watching dolphins head down the coast toward San Diego. Having walked along this track for many years, I recognize people I meet. I spotted a woman with a dog who looked familiar. She stopped when she saw me. As I bent down to give her dog a good pat, she asked if I was the woman who had told her about using coconut oil for seizures. I nodded. She told me that, ever since she started giving her dog a tablespoon of coconut oil a day, he has not had a seizure. I thought, *If only it had that result for Ebony.*

March 16: Stefan Called to Tell Me That Ebony Was Urinating in the House

Sometimes, she did it right after they'd been outside. I asked if he noticed any blood, in which case it might be another bladder infection. A day later, he called to say he did see blood. I suggested giving her cranberry pills and asking the vet to renew the antibiotic medication. After Ebony took the medicine, the problem cleared up quickly.

April 7: Finally, Spring

Cool air caressing my face and the sun already higher in the sky warms my back as Ebie and I ascend the trail. All around, a symphony of bird calls. It's time to build nests and nurture offspring. Ebony's doing fine. As we eat outside enjoying the breeze before the summer humidity arrives, Ebony sits with us. As always, she's waiting to see what food we'll share with her. Sometimes, she wanders off to take care of business. She knows to go to our lot next door rather than do anything in the immediate yard. No seizures since early March.

April 14: Confusion

We went for a walk down by the creek where we passed several people with dogs, and as usual, they commented on Ebie's good looks. One person with two dogs stopped to talk with us. Sam, the dog on the outside, came up to sniff, but Ebie turned her head away. I explained to the man that given her age, she no longer has any interest in greeting other dogs. He asked how old she is, and when I answered she would turn fourteen in September, he said, "Wow, she looks great."

I replied she has her problems. He commented, "Just like us." I agreed, but I was thinking that at least we can describe our problems—Ebie can't. As we continued, she poked along, her breathing labored. When we got to the loop and crossed the creek, she started running back up the path where we'd started. Luckily, we caught her before she got to the road. However, we wondered why this change and confusion.

Her running toward home reminded me of how horses pick up their pace when they're heading back to the stable. My first lesson with this routine was when I was a student having just finished my junior year abroad. Our group ended the year in Holland at a resort called Nordwijck am See. After, I visited London; I headed back to Holland and the resort by the sea. I had spotted people riding horses along the seashore, and since I was a good rider, I thought it would be a special experience to ride along a beach. The hotel directed me to the stables. The manager, a young man, lent me riding boots. It was a great ride, and I settled in. A German man and his daughter were also on the sunset ride, and we chatted briefly as our horses trotted along the beach.

After thirty minutes, we turned away from the shore and came to a small restaurant that had a wooden post outside for tying up the horses. We all went inside and enjoyed a beer. Then came time to ride back to the stable. Now, the sun was setting, and our horses trotted along the jagged edge of the beach partially in the water. Suddenly, my horse lifted his head high as if about to whinny and then quickly changed gates to a canter. It was difficult to keep him from getting his head and thundering along the water's edge all the way home. Nevertheless, I managed.

Sometimes, the moments that scare you are the most enjoyable. Later, the manager of the stables confirmed that his horses know when they're going home, and if you aren't careful, they will gallop like a racehorse all the way back.

May 2: Neurology and Idiopathic Epilepsy

Since our regular vet really couldn't help us as Ebony's condition advanced, we took her to a neurologist. He watched Ebony for a while, and she watched him. She was comfortable in his office and moved around looking out the window and wondering why we'd brought her here. He said idiopathic epilepsy is a condition sometimes common in younger dogs. When dogs become Ebie's age and begin having seizures, the condition is usually caused by something else. I wonder whether our vet has been trying to spare us from the truth all this time.

While we were watching Ebony, she crossed her front legs as she'd been doing lately, and the neurologist pointed to it. He said something in her brain is getting signals mixed up. He went to Ebony and put his head to hers. Then he asked if he could examine her and get her to lie on the floor. We agreed. He got down himself on all fours and turned Ebony over. Ebony didn't resist him, but she probably wondered what game he wanted to play. He commented on how smart poodles are. In fact, he said, "Poodles don't get enough credit. They are very resilient dogs." He suggested blood tests, but said he was sure it was brain related. Given her age of thirteen, he understood that we would not want to subject her to surgery if she has a tumor.

The shock and sad news came when he said her medication should be dramatically higher based on her weight. We were giving her 50 mg twice a day or 100 mg total, and when we thought, she was approaching the cycle we increased it. However, he said, based on her weight, it should be 400 mg a day. We asked if dramatically increasing the medication would slow her down to a state of sleep. He responded that if her condition is brain related, the increased medication could switch off her attentiveness, and she might be far less alert.

We decided to only give her 300 (150 twice a day). The increase does slow her down. Now, she sleeps most of the day, only waking up to eat. She continues to have a hearty appetite. We worry because sometimes she only pees and poops once a day. We have to walk her around and around. A few times, she pooped in the house right after we brought her in from outside. She also increasingly appears to be in her own world.

May 27: Where Does Her Strength Come From?

On Saturday, we started to lower her medication to just 100 twice a day, and as a result, we think we detected more energy and life in her step. We went down to the park, and she ran a good piece. At 4:30 a.m., she had her first seizure since March. So far, there has only been one. We walked her outside for more than thirty minutes because she was so hyperactive. We could barely keep her steady she pulled so hard to go wherever she wanted. Where does that strength come from at such an advanced age? The results of the blood test were all perfect, indicating a healthy dog with no signs of regression or weakness. All the categories were within normal range.

At 11:50 a.m., she had another seizure. This time, she cried as she had in March. She had another at 8:30 p.m. It was short. Stefan decided to sleep downstairs in the guest bedroom and kept her bed in the area in front of the bathroom. She had another seizure around 1:00 a.m. and then another at 5:30 a.m. The seizures were initially eight hours apart, but as of the morning of the twenty-eighth, they were five and four hours apart.

At 12:00 p.m., Stefan called me at work to tell me she had another seizure (six and a half hours apart). I came home early, and she had another at 5:20 p.m. I was alone with her, and she started to cry about two hours later and bark. Poor little girl. Usually, giving her food helps to calm her down and stop the barking. Once the seizures started, we went back to the 150 mg twice a day. Now it's difficult to give her the medication after a seizure. Unlike the Ebony who carefully avoids biting our fingers in play even in the heat of a game, the Ebony after seizures has become feral, and several times, she has bitten down hard on our fingers.

She had yet another at 10:30 p.m. and on May 29 at 4:40 a.m. and at 9:50 a.m. (ten so far). At 6:00 p.m., she had number eleven, and fortunately, that ended the period except for weakness, poor balance, and lack of orientation that takes about four days before she gets back to normal. Once again, it was a bonding experience. She had become so distant and sometimes moved away when we tried to pat her. But during her desperation, especially one or two hours after a seizure when she whines and barks, she looks up with complete trust and love and wants to be comforted. One cannot forget those looks and moments of affection we share.

June 10: Pet Sematary

Stefan thought she would never recover, but yesterday, we went for a walk down to the creek, and she did just fine. She has regained her balance. She eats as if she's been starving. Her biological functions have changed. She only does one long pee a day. More alarming is that like the story line in Stephen King's book *Pet Sematary*, every time she goes through one of the episodes, she returns to us changed. Each time she loses some of her spirit. She looks like Ebie and has the same beautiful features. She sits paws crossed like a princess.

However, when you try to come close to hug or pet her, she now gets up to move to another location. Sometimes when we wake her, she looks up surprised, as if to say, "Who are you?" We aren't sure she recognizes us, but we regain her trust each day because she knows we're feeding her and are attentive to her needs. No more kisses, even when I stroke her when she's lying down. She has developed the habit of eating her food in a reclining position, and her breathing when she walks is labored.

She has also developed a very stubborn streak. She doesn't want to follow outside if we want her to go for a short walk along the trail. Unless we take her by her collar or halter, she tries to turn quickly and walk fast in the other direction. Lately, when we grab her quickly, she turns her head fast as if ready to bite us. We've never seen her act this way. In addition, she's been a very clean dog about where she does her business, except during a seizure when she can't control what she does. However, lately, she's been compulsively going to the front of the house and leaving poop right in front of the door for us to see.

This morning, she was especially confused and less responsive to us. We insisted she go on a short walk along the path behind the house. Once we got going, she seemed to enjoy sniffing. Don't underestimate the importance of sniffing—it helps your dog wake up because they're processing information.

After some good sniffing, she was more cooperative and more herself. She went by herself to the lot and did a long pee.

July 15: Compulsive Behavior

She's much better, but she jitters a lot (jerkies). Research tells us each jerk is a form of seizure. Therefore, she's having seizures all the time. The bad ones are the grand mal. Sometimes, she walks like a drunken sailor and seems confused. The pattern of walking to the front of the house, standing on the stoop, and surveying up and down the street is becoming acute. Whenever we sit outside to have dinner, she makes several trips to the front of the house. When I appear around the corner to check on her, she comes over and follows me to the back of the house again. She no longer likes to lie down. Perhaps it hurts her? Ironically, she's getting more exercise with all the trips she makes to the front of the house. Her trips are compulsive and remind one of dementia.

August 4: We Lost Her

Today, we were walking down the path by the stream. I had her off the leash so she could do some good sniffing. I looked back, and she stared at me. I turned to keep walking and then after a few feet turned again. She was gone. It struck me that she might be running all the way back to the car. I began running and called out to Stefan. She was nowhere in sight. I got to the car, and she wasn't there either. Stefan said he would drive around, and I should keep walking toward home. She wasn't at home when I got there and Stefan drove up.

He got in the car again and, this time, drove in the other direction in case she'd turned left instead of right by the park entrance. He came back without her. He said he had spoken to some people walking a white poodle. They said they saw her cross the creek. The stepping-stones going across the creek are halfway down the path. She hadn't gone straight up the hill toward the car.

Stefan headed toward the other entrance to the park and spotted a woman with a leash in her hand, and then he spotted Ebie. The woman said she knew something was wrong because our dog had come as far as her house three times and then gone back down the trail. While Stefan was relieved to find her, Ebie seemed unfazed except for being out of breath. What a rascal. The sad part of the incident is that her behavior indicates she's becoming confused about things that should be familiar.

Sep 15: Zonisamide Has Soared in Price

We wanted to renew Ebie's prescription for Zonisamide. By taking out a plan at Walgreens, we saved good money over the course of the year. Two hundred of the 50 mg tablets ran about thirty dollars. However, when we went to renew, they told us the price was $136 after the discount. How can the cost of medicine quadruple in less than six months? The last time I had picked it up was in April. Fortunately, we found that Costco sold the same medication for a much better price, and it wasn't necessary to take out a plan.

September 23: Compulsive Circling

There's no doubt now that Ebie has developed a compulsive routine of circling the house. If we sit outside, she starts. We count each trip. For example, here she comes for the fifth time. She can circle at least eight-to-ten times. On each cycle, she stops at the front landing and looks up and down the street. Almost daily, she leaves a present in front of the door. When she's ready to come in, she goes to the back door and just stands there. She's set in this routine and dislikes being interrupted. She pulls away or runs from you if you try to stop her. If you try to pet her, she ducks to the side.

September 29: Ebony Has Turned Fourteen

What an amazing dog. She eats like a horse, but according to the scale at the vet, she's losing weight. On our last visit, her thyroid level was low, and now we have her on thyroid medication. Our vet has warned us that although she's still physically strong, things are going downhill. He urges us to make a decision, saying that most people who wait wish they'd made the decision earlier. Think of the dog and what pain they might face and how you'll remember them. It's a quality-of-life issue for the dog as well as the owner.

LAST ANNIVERSARY

October 2013—December 2013

Autumn Leaves

It's a beautiful autumn. Although Stefan and I are enjoying delicious cold cider that speaks of bright foliage and sunny, crisp days, we're saddened about our companion, Ebony. Her actions over the past few months demonstrate all the characteristics of dementia. She has changed dramatically ever since the visit to the neurologist. We can no longer keep her with us at night. We must confine her to Stefan's office. We find a mess each morning, and she doesn't seem to recognize us when she wakes up.

Why has it come to this? Based on our vet's advice, we've decided, but we haven't agreed on a date. Stefan will soon be off to Europe. I'll remain with Ebony. Since we might not have her much longer, we would be uncomfortable if we both left. There is only a week between Stefan's return and my trip to Cyprus, where I serve as an advisor for an EU-funded digital cultural heritage project. We both want to be with her when the time comes.

October 5: She Is Lost to Us Now

Outside, Ebony is strong, circling the house several times in good stride. When we sit outside, she tries to alter her routine path to shy away from us. She still accepts food from us when we hold it out, and, most of the time, she'll allow us to administer her pills. Today, she was restless again and paced back and forth inside the house like a caged lion. I was in the kitchen while she paced from inside Stefan's office to the kitchen and back. I sat down on the floor to see what she would do. She looked at me with some curiosity, but would not approach. Despite these disturbing signs, I often wrap my arms around her and say behind her ear so she can hear me, "Ebie is a very good dog." I don't know if she still understands me, but it helps me deal with the situation, thinking she just might understand. She does respond to her name if you say it very loud.

We've stopped taking her for a haircut. At the salon, she used to step up on the pedestal proudly, as if to say, "I know this routine." Now, she twists and struggles to get away from Hindi because she doesn't like to be touched. It's impossible to cut her hair. Nevertheless, to us she's still loveable. I melt when I feel her soft breath over my hand as I hold out something for her to eat. Stefan wishes her a good night each evening and has a little talk with her. We try to spoil her by giving her cooked chopped meat and steak. She still has a good appetite, and we still keep her bowl close to us in the dining room, so we can share our meals together. It's one way to keep her socialized.

October 17: What to Do? What to Do?

Stefan's in Europe, and I think of this as my last time alone with Ebie. It breaks my heart. She no longer comes upstairs. We always used to check on each other. At night, I would wake, and, almost simultaneously, she would awaken as well and turn her head to see what I was doing. Then both of us would fall back to sleep. Now, I study her, hoping for a sign that indicates she might snap back. However, the whittling away of her spirit hasn't left much hope.

October 18: A Sign of Intelligence

I was taken aback today when I witnessed her engaging in a very clever move. I sat on the floor again, hoping she would come over to me. She was pacing, as usual, like a lion in a cage. I'd closed the door to Stefan's office to see what she would do. Ebie began jiggling the handle with her nose until it unlatched, and she was able to push in the door and enter the office. How can she be so smart on the one hand and yet in another world mentally? Perhaps the two are not connected.

Now, she sleeps only in Stefan's office, where she urinates and poops. Each morning, we enter the office not knowing what we will find. It's Stefan who normally takes care of the mess. Now, it's my turn. I notice that when she wakes, the first thing she does is look outside. Perhaps each time she wakes, she's unsure of where and who she is. She certainly doesn't look at us with any recognition. My first move is to open the door from his office that leads outside, and she immediately chooses to go out and start the circles around the house. In the meantime, the room needs to be cleaned. When the weather is warm enough, I remove the entire tarp from the floor, place it on the hillside, and hose it down. A clean tarp is put in its place. The tarp and floor are cleaned with white vinegar and water. It's a sad situation, and even more disturbing is the fact that she hasn't had a seizure since May (five months).

November 19: The Confusion Has Gotten Worse

Now, there are signs of confusion even within her compulsive patterns. This afternoon, we wondered where she was because she didn't cross the backyard in her routine trips around the house. Then, we found her below the front stone wall, just standing there, staring. How she got there we don't know. The other night, she also disappeared. It was toward dusk. We got our flashlights to search for her. I called our neighbor, who fosters dogs, and he found her between his house and the next neighbor. She forgot to make the turn at the side of our house when she crossed our front steps; instead, she was two houses down from ours. To make matters even more heartbreaking, sometimes she still prances as if she were a show dog on the runway.

We observed Ebie's three-year anniversary since the seizures started. It was Thanksgiving in 2010, a few days after we'd arrived in Beijing. Now, there's no climbing up on the living room sofa to watch us like a little mouse. No climbing the stairs to visit me in my office. No games and eyes flashing with excitement. No wagging tails and kisses. No greeting us and squeezing through our legs. Nevertheless, she is still gentle with us and breathes softly.

November 24: Realization

Although she's more confused, she never snarls or bares her teeth. Today, she made several jumps over the logs that straddle the trail to keep it from eroding, and she ran home when we got to the bottom. Her appetite is still very good, and although she continues to lose weight, she appears physically stronger. She has difficulty settling down and stands most of the time. We met with our vet, and we talked. He suggested giving us some sleeping pills when the time comes, so that we can give them to her before we bring her to his office. By making her drowsy, she won't recognize and react to the surroundings. He told us we were making the right decision. He said the weight loss was also an indication that she has a condition that, in all likelihood, would soon take her life. When I mentioned that, despite all the problems over the past few years with her joints, she's now jumping over logs, he said that her mind's probably so gone that she doesn't remember she has arthritis.

November 26: A Question of Dignity

Stefan said the other day there's no way to return to a more normal time. She's not going to start wagging her tail or remember to go when we take her outside. Moreover, there's the question of dignity. She looks like Ebie, but she's not the same dog. I fear she's frightened. Imagine waking up each day and not knowing who these people around you are. Are we keeping her for ourselves and avoiding the finality of letting her go? She eats and sleeps and still can jump and run. Is she comfortable, or is she frightened? What's fair to her?

Our vet said that when you find them staring at the wall, it's time. We have found her just standing in the middle of the room, not sure what she wants to do. This morning, she ran away from us. She mainly stares at me as if she's trying to figure out who I am. When I move closer, she quickly moves away.

We still have her eat with us, placing her food and water stand near our dining room table. Occasionally, she leans close to me to sniff my plate, and in those moments, I relive how it used to be with her, outside, on top of the hill of the trail, standing together and protecting each other. I always have enjoyed sharing such moments with my dog or horse. Sometimes you feel closer to nature when you experience it with an animal. It deepens the experience.

December 2: We've Made the Decision. God Help Us!

We miss her already. We took her for a walk today, and another person stopped to say, "What a beautiful dog." When I said she was over fourteen, they replied, "Well, she looks great." She had a good stride the entire way, although it was longer than usual and she leaned into me, perhaps as a sign of affection. However, between her walk this morning and noon, she defecated on her bed and laid in it, not even realizing she was lying in her own poop. We won't enjoy walks for a long time without her striding at our side. Nevertheless, it's not fair to such a majestic and noble companion to let her go on just for our sake

Our vet said when they begin to fail, it can go very fast, and most people wish they'd made the decision earlier. She led a very good life, and we went through hell with her for three years with seizures coming every several weeks. Ironically, those stopped, and there hasn't been one for seven months. She's still so sweet when she eats with us. We'll give her a sedative two hours before we take her to the vet. We hope it will be a peaceful ending. There's no doubt we'll shed many tears, because they've already begun.

December 4: We Will Always Love You

Almost to the date when it all started, our beautiful companion has been put to rest. You just never think you'll outlive them. Although Ebony slept most of the time this past year, the house seems unusually quiet. In the end, it went as uneventfully as we could have hoped. We'd decided not to have the vet I met come to the house to administer the injection. She would have been a stranger to Ebony and might have caused some chaos. Our regular vet suggested tranquilizers that would subdue Ebony so that she wouldn't notice she was at the vet.

This morning, she ate a hearty breakfast with leftover steak, and we went for a walk. She was calm and kept close. Our vet gave us two pills, but only one was needed. She was so relaxed that we had trouble getting her into the car. She slept so peacefully, only looking up when they shaved her arm for the medication. We both wept. I couldn't help myself and fell to my knees and wept over her body, which was stretched out on the gurney in our vet's office. I inhaled the woodsy-and-lavender scent of her fur one last time.

Ironically, as I left to go out the front door while Stefan went out the back with Ebie wrapped in a bundle, I saw a man sitting, with a black puppy hiding behind his leg. It looked like a poodle. I asked, and he said, "She's a standard." With tears streaking down my cheeks, I informed him that we'd just put our poodle, Ebony, to sleep. The little one that he called Bella looked up at me, wagging her tail. I wished Bella a good life and left.

December 14: Torment

Our decision was not made lightly. We routinely investigated articles about epilepsy, seizures, and dementia affecting dogs. Our vet was signaling us that it was time. As we were waiting for Ebony to pass forever into sleep, after he administered the shot, he repeated, "It was the right decision or I wouldn't have recommended it." Yet we find ourselves questioning the decision. We wish we had sought opinions about her condition from other veterinarians and tried various seizure medications. We miss her and hope we spared her from agony that was to come. Saying goodbye is never easy. As I used to tell her, "We will love you always." And so we will.

December 21: So Many Fond Memories

As the days go, by our eyes are often wet, as so many little things remind us of our little girl. When Stefan rakes leaves, he thinks of her circling the house. Our hearts ache when we find early photos depicting a stunning dog of top showmanship. What makes us particularly sad is how happy she looks in those early days. She has that wonderful smile, shining eyes, and elegant poses—either standing like a thoroughbred horse with one leg forward, or reclining in the grass with her long legs crossed in front of her, her lively eyes drawing you in.

Whenever we have dinner, we think of how we prepared her bowl and placed it on her eating stand near the dining room table, and if there are leftovers, we think of how much she enjoyed sharing dinner with us. It is heart-wrenching. We still question whether we made the right decision. Since her physical strength was improving, was there any chance she might have gotten better? Then we remember that, although she was more active, she was driven and not connecting with us. If I sat next to her bed in Stefan's office and stroked her, she would get up to leave the room. The real Ebony left us several months ago.

Woolly girl
"We love you"

EPILOGUE

December 24—January 1, 2014

Holding back the tears day in and day out, there was a bright spot when a little Portuguese water dog spent the Christmas holidays with us. Less than half the size of Ebie, she stood erect, looking ready and able. She was as cute as could be with her Groucho Marx eyebrows, short ears, curly black fur, white chest, and a sprinkle of white around one side of her nose that looked like she'd just sniffed flour. What a character. At first, she was polite and very quiet. I was taken aback when she started licking my cheek and followed me everywhere I went. To get our attention, she made a high-pitched treble sound that sounded like the language of the Ewoks in *Star Wars*.

The night she arrived, she disappeared for a brief time while we were discussing her diet with her owners. We all turned when we heard her romping down the stairs. The little rascal had already inspected the upper level of our house, and I guess we passed. As the days went by, she brought so much life back into our home that one could not have wished for a nicer Christmas gift. There was raucous play, hide-and-seek, tossing toys into the air, snortling, looking out the window for us to come home, and, when we came through the door, the beating of her tail against our paper shopping bags—and much more. It was a joy.

Now we know that, someday, there will be another dog who we will love. However, in our hearts, we acknowledge that there will always be only one Ebony.

There will always be only one Ebony

Recommendations

If your pet is sick, don't scold them for accidents that may occur over which they have no control. Pets feel badly when they do something wrong. They know they disappointed you.

Unless your vet recommends otherwise, try keeping to regular activities such as taking your pet outdoors for short walks. Sniffing stimulates their brain activity.

Communicate with your pet on a regular basis; calm them if they appear nervous; assure your pet that you love him or her.

If administering pills is problematic, try slipping the pill inside some chopped meat or peanut butter. However, be aware that too large a ball of peanut butter could lodge in the throat and your dog could choke.

Note that some stores offer a prescription plan for pets. You join the plan, and then pay far less as you fill a prescription. A good example is Walgreens. We found Costco has the lowest prices, and there's no need to join a plan.

If your pet suffers from arthritis, ask your vet if it is OK to line your pet's bed with memory foam.

If your pet sleeps on your bed or close to it and suffers from seizures or has bladder problems, cover the area with a plastic sheet or shower curtain and place an old cotton sheet for comfort on top of it. Both the plastic and the cotton sheet are easy to wash. You can also use disposal bed mats. Keep old towels nearby for cleaning up accidents.

If there's an accident on wooden or tile floors, try using white vinegar with water to cleanse the area.

Buy a harness that wraps around your dog's girth and has a handle you can hold. It will help you move your dog up and down stairs and keep your dog from falling over after seizures. The harness not only helps you control your dog, but may also make your dog feel better and more secure.

You should follow your vet's recommended dosage for epilepsy. If you see a pattern emerge for the seizures, ask if it would be OK to increase the dosage a few days before the cycle begins.

If your dog suffers from clusters of seizures, becomes very weak, and has difficulty standing, be patient. Wait a few days to see if the condition improves.

If you're unsure about the treatment your vet recommends, consider obtaining a second opinion. The Cornell School of Veterinary Medicine may also prove helpful for comparing notes. It has sections on health topics, research, diagnostics, and hospitals. https://www2.vet.cornell.edu/

Talk to your dog and judge whether he or she recognizes you.

If your vet tells you there's nothing more they can do, ask yourself if the dog still has good days. There's an old saying that your pet will let you know when the time has come. If the good days are few, and if you think your pet is scared, confused, doesn't recognize you, pulls away and doesn't want to be touched, just stares into space for long periods of time, is suffering from pain, and so on, it may be time to discuss with your vet what would be a comfortable way for both you and your pet to say goodbye.

If it's time, try to either find a vet who will come to your house or ask your vet for sleeping pills so that your dog isn't aware of what's happening and remains calm.

Just like people, every pet is special. Although the loss will hurt, focus on the good days you and your pet enjoyed together.

If you feel strongly that there will never be another pet like the one you lost, consider taking care of a friend's or neighbor's pet for a few days. You may rediscover the joy of pet companionship.

Good luck.

Made in the USA
Las Vegas, NV
14 December 2020

13105114R00083